Golden Goddess and Bloody Times

By P F Jeffery

London
Tuerqui's Treasure Books
2010

The Warriors of Love Volume 5 Tuerqui
By P. F. Jeffery

ISBN 978-1-4457-5001-9

First Edition 2010

© P. F. Jeffery

Tuerqui's Treasure Books
Published by P F Jeffery

Front cover photograph: P Madden

By the same author

Already published:

Jane: The Warriors of Love Volume 1
Margaret: The Warriors of Love Volume 2
Tuerqui: The Warriors of Love Volume 5

To be published later in 2010:

Margaret Again: The Warriors of Love Volume 8

Projected for 2011:

Tuerqui Again: The Warriors of Love Volume 11

For subsequent publication:

The Warriors of Love volumes 3, 4, 6, 7, 9, 10 and 12

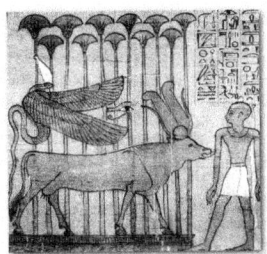

Contents

Look what they done to my song, Ma
Look what they done to my song
Well, it's the only thing I could do half right
And it's turning out all wrong, Ma
Look what they done to my song

Look what they done to my brain, Ma
Look what they done to my brain
Well, they picked it like a chicken bone
And I think I'm half insane, Ma
Look what they done to my brain

– Melanie Safka

It isn't there now, but there used to be a poster at my local station, advertising an airline:

You are here
Why?

The question seemed worth an answer. My first response was *because I live here*. But, looking anew at the poster every evening on my way home, I realised that the answer depended on what it meant by *here*. My first thought had been that *here* was the general locality – perhaps half a mile or a mile's radius from the station. My second thought was that *here* might be more narrowly defined – the station, or even just its eastbound platform. Taking that as the meaning, the answer had to do with my being on my way home from work (and where I worked and where I live).

Not until later did it occur to me that *here* might be taken as having wider reference: *why I am I here, in this world.* (There seems something significant in this being the last of the three interpretations to occur to me.) The answer to that final interpretation, it seemed to me – as I jostled through the crowd towards the stairs, the ticket barrier and the street – had to do with my parents having sex on a certain date. If my mental arithmetic is correct, it was in October 1945. Since my father had been a prisoner of war, the answer to *why I am I here, in this world* can be extended from the sexual act itself to something about the course of the Second World War. It might take in the timing of when the American army reached Bavaria, and how quickly they repatriated prisoners of war. The Soviet victories at Stalingrad and Kursk paved the way to my birth… and to my 1950s upbringing, which has much to do with the nature of the *I* the new born babe was destined to become.

It was only in the calm of a side street that I realised that many people would give a very different answer to *why I am I here, in this world.* Quite a lot would seek an answer in the presumed purposes of their deity. My answer, rooted in sex, would seem – by their standards – non-religious. The more I thought about it, the question of whether my sexual answer was non-religious depends on what one's religion makes of sex. In Christian mythology, sex is presented as a rather mucky add-on to the process of divine creation. In Kemetic (ancient Egyptian) myth, it is the engine that drives the process of divine creation. I know which of those makes more sense to me.

Maybe it depends on how one defines the phrase *divine creation.* Is it a single act at the first time – something that set the universe in motion? Or is it a continuing process – something ongoing, that is still with us? Is deity akin to someone who winds up a clock and then lets it run? Or is deity constantly encountered in the world? If the latter, sex certainly seems to be the mechanism through which divine creation takes place.

Universes Living and Dead

There is, of course, a question as to whether there is (or ever has been) such a thing as divine creation. There is a mechanistic view of the universe, taking the first creation as an entirely impersonal big bang. In its most extreme form, adherents of this view interpret everything that has happened since the big bang as the working out of impersonal forces.

In a less extreme form, the mechanistic view makes an exception for our own species – allowing us free will to shape (in some wise) our own creations. Immanuel Kant wrote a short book, the title of which may be translated as *The Fundamental Principles of the Metaphysics of Morals* (different translations have slightly different titles). In this brief work, Kant advances the idea that we can only exercise free will by acting morally. If we do not act morally, Kant argued, we act purely according to our desires – and these desires are determined mechanistically. This seems to echo a number of ideas found in Buddhism – including a negative view of desire.

This mechanistic view, taking on board free will, assumes that there is an enormous gulf between us and all of the other creatures on the face of this planet. The same, no doubt, goes for most religious viewpoints. Having the pleasure and privilege of living with a cat, I don't think this can be justified. It seems to me that my cat makes decisions in a very similar way to me. We are, clearly, similar creatures. Every bone in our bodies has an equivalent in the other's body. The things that make us the same are more numerous and significant than the things that make us different.

Long ago, cats and people had common ancestors. Did some of the descendants of these ancestors (*our* ancestors) suddenly acquire free will – while others did not (*the cats'* ancestors)? What was that strange event (the emergence of free will)? How did it happen? Was a creature, whose parents didn't have free will, born with free will? Did the creature acquire free will after birth? Was the free will thereafter transmitted genetically to its descendants? Can we transmit genetically anything with which we are not born?

I feel easier with the idea of a purely mechanistic universe than I do with the idea of the universe as a machine from which we are (partly) excluded. The latter is special pleading. *Of course that doesn't apply to my species* is an extension (on a grander scale) of the familiar line: *of course that doesn't apply to me.* I think (for example) of the bosses who insist on pay restraint *although of course that doesn't apply to me.*

3

The question of whether the universe is a machine – or filled with (composed of?) spirits – can be rephrased as the question of whether the universe is living or dead. Both the living and the dead universes seem to me tenable constructions on the observable world. In favour of the living universe, I advance merely that it seems to agree better with my experience of the world

Kemetic Rationalism

The view to which my experiences (and intuitions) lead me is something for which the world in general seems to have no handy word or phrase. I have felt the necessity to coin my own term: Kemetic Rationalism.

Kemetic stems from the ancient Egyptians' name for their country *Kemet*. I take the adjective *Kemetic* from a group of people (based in America) who describe their religion as *Kemetic Orthodox*. By this they mean that they have adopted – as nearly as it is possible to do so – the religion of ancient Egypt. I add the qualification *as nearly as it is possible to do so* because Kemetic religion was destroyed by the rise of the aggressive and intolerant cult of Christianity. And (obviously) there are no ancient Egyptians left to consult on religious matters (or on anything else, if it comes to that).

In the year 1800, no one knew very much about Kemetic religion. Nobody was able to read the scripts of ancient Egypt. The only evidences for Kemetic religion were the writings of Hellenes and Romans – and what could be inferred from Egyptian art and other physical remains.

It is evidently true that some Hellenic and Roman writers spoke with Egyptian priests, but what they tell us should not be accepted uncritically. One problem is that what they have to tell us does not reflect Egyptian civilisation at its zenith, but comes from a period of decline and increasing foreign influence. In fact, followers of the Kemetic Orthodoxy specifically discount late Egyptian writings, feeling that the religion of the time had been debased by foreign influences.

A further problem with the accounts of Hellenes and Romans is that they viewed late Kemetic religion through the filters of their own assumptions. Were we able to speak directly to those late Kemetic priests, our impressions of their religion would undoubtedly be significantly different from the impressions of Hellenic and Roman authors. Nor do we know for how long or in what depth the Hellenic and Roman writers spoke to the Egyptian priests. For the most part, I suspect, the conversations were brief and superficial. The conversations, moreover, are likely to have been conducted through interpreters – giving plenty of scope for misunderstanding. It is also doubtful whether they asked the questions we would wish to ask.

If the accounts of Hellenic and Roman writers are heavy with misinterpretation, how much more so were early attempts to interpret artistic and other physical remains of the vanished civilisation? There are numerous false impressions about Kemetic religion that one might draw from physical remains. For example, Kemetic iconography often depicts deities as animal-headed people.

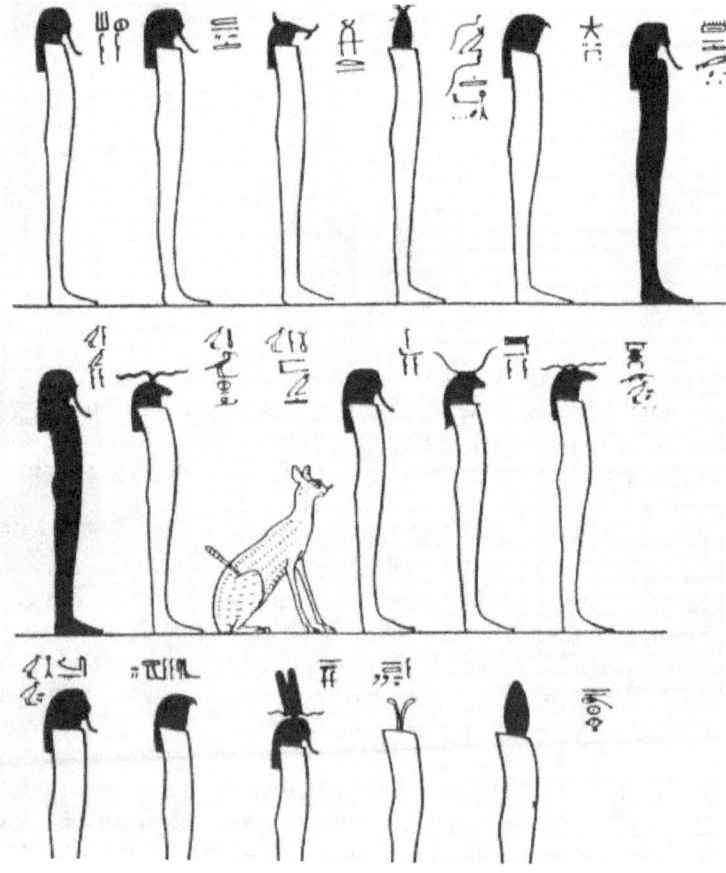

It might be supposed that deities are actually imagined to have such an appearance. In fact, of course, we cannot directly see divinities at all – and they do not, as such, have any appearance. Depicting goddesses or gods with human bodies allows them, without difficulty, to be shown as performing actions. It is, for this reason, a useful convention. (The actions they are shown as undertaking are – in the nature of things – generally symbolic. For example, a divinity may be shown presenting an ankh – the hieroglyph for *life* – to a person. This represents the deity giving life.) The animal heads make some kind of statement about the goddess or god depicted. They have to do with the association of the deity with the animal and with shared qualities between animal and divinity. Since these images can act as a body for the deity, giving the goddess or god a continued presence in a specific place, the images need to be harmonious to be effective – and to be pleasing to the divinity in question.

In the year 1900, we still knew too little about Kemetic religion for anyone – in a meaningful sense – to adopt it. Over the last eighty years or so, there had been enormous gains in our knowledge of the ancient cultures of the Nile. Scholars could now translate ancient Egyptian texts, albeit sometimes with renditions that are now no longer acceptable.

There was a second block to the understanding of scholars in 1900 – a general inability to place preconceptions to one side. Hellenic and Roman writers had spoken with Egyptian priests, filtering what they heard through the assumptions of the classical world. Too many of the scholars of 1900 filtered their findings through a set of assumptions further removed from those of the Egyptian priests – assumptions blended from Christianity and nineteenth century science (a pair of uneasy bed fellows).

By the year 2000, we had started to know enough about Kemetic religion for someone – in a meaningful sense – to adopt it. Most certainly, the bulk of what we knew about ancient Egypt and its religion had been discovered in the last hundred years. Arguably, most of it had been discovered in the last fifty years. Although there have been new archaeological discoveries in Egypt – some of them important – they are not the major factor in the advance of our knowledge. More significantly, scholars have re-evaluated the existing evidence. An important part of this has been philological work – gaining a better understanding of the ancient Egyptian language. Just as significant as the linguistic work, I think, is the way in which many scholars have actively attempted to put to one side their preconceptions. A more phenomenological approach (of which more later) has yielded a much better understanding of things that (in theory) we already knew.

It would be wrong to say that we are entirely familiar with the religion – or, indeed, that we will ever know it completely. However, we do now know it sufficiently well for someone (in a meaningful sense) to adopt it.

Actually, I doubt whether it is possible for anyone to be completely familiar with any religion. Religion is about the unknowable. To know it fully would be to turn it into something other than religion.

So – for the first time in almost two millennia, Kemetic religion is – in its essence – available to those who would seek it... Or those whom the Kemetic deities would seek... So much for the *Kemetic* part of *Kemetic rationalism*, what of the *rationalism*? At first sight, rationalism might seem to sit uneasily with the religion of ancient Egypt.

My first thought on this is that it would be more uneasy for a follower of the Kemetic religion to adopt a point of view that denied or opposed rationalism. Unlike religions with an unbroken history since their inception, Kemetic religion depends on rationalism to reveal it. The decipherment of hieroglyphs belongs to the age of reason – and every extension in our knowledge since then has depended upon the exercise of reason.

A further thought is that our reason is a gift from the gods – and, if the gods did not wish us to use it, they surely would not have given it to us.

Beyond this, it seems to me that Kemetic religion sits more easily with rationalism than any other set of religious ideas of which I am aware. The absolutism characteristic of most religions is alien to the Kemetic outlook. The religion functions on a multi-value logic that can embrace both the rational and irrational. It did so in ancient times and it can do so now. I hope that this will become clear in the explorations that follow – explorations of abstract ideas, of my personal history, and of the way I perceive the world to be.

Through and Beyond Christianity

I was brought up to be some kind of Christian. I don't think, though, that the religion ever did make sense to me. The basic tenet seems to be that the world was redeemed through the crucifixion of Jesus. I've never had the least idea in what way this event was supposed to make anything better. I don't think that I even understand (or ever understood) what *redeemed* can mean in the context of *the world was redeemed*. I can understand that when I behave badly I can redeem myself by doing something especially good. But if the world was to be redeemed in this sense, surely the whole world would have to do something especially good. That is because *to redeem* (in this sense) seems to be a very unusual verb in that the subject and object are, of necessity, the same. I can redeem myself. You can redeem yourself – but I can't redeem you, or you me. And, come to that, what has the world (as such) ever done wrong? People behave wrongly – and may or may not be able to redeem themselves afterwards, but the world? As far as I can see, the concept just doesn't make any sense at all.

Another sense of *redeemed* seems, at first, to make even less sense: that of redeeming a pawn ticket. Well – a life as the price of retrieving the world from some kind of cosmic hock is comprehensible as an idea. I could even imagine three of the planets forming the pawnbroker's sign. (Or three of Jupiter's moons, when correctly aligned?) But who is the cosmic pawnbroker? – some kind of deity, I suppose. More puzzling is the question of who placed the world in hock. It seems to require a second deity to perform such a feat. And what would the deity have received from the pawnbroker in return for pledging the world? Somehow, in contemplating such transactions, one might expect more than a single life to be necessary to redeem so large an object as the world. And does the resurrection business mean that the cosmic pawnbroker was bilked? That sense of *redeemed* turns out not make a lot of sense, either – but it may, in spite of first appearances, make more sense than that of redeeming oneself after behaving badly.

Near the tail end of a large book by Jan Assman, I found something that might throw some light on the business of redemption:

If the Egyptian encounter with Hellenism was particularly fertile, the confrontation with Christianity could not have been more devastating. The demise of Egyptian civilization as a semantic universe was a direct result of the advent of the redemptive religions. To the very end the unshakable convictions that informed Egyptian theology – especially in its Greek forms of hermeticism, Neoplatonism and alchemy – were that man is at home in the world, that human participation is essential to the divine scheme of sustaining the world, and that the unending task of reconciling the human and the divine is the true source of worldly coherence and continuity. The longing to be redeemed from this world instead of being piously incorporated into it was completely alien to Egyptian thought.

– Jan Assman *The Mind of Egypt* Harvard University Press paperback, 2003. pp 424-425

The longing to be redeemed from this world instead of being piously incorporated into it is completely alien not only to Egyptian thought but to mine as well. What Jan Assman has to say on this matter does little, if anything, to help me comprehend the redemption business. It does, however, confirm that this issue is central to my inability to comprehend Christianity.

I have tried to make sense of stuff that Christians seem to accept without question, and not made much headway.

If I can't make head nor tail of Christianity, it is not the religion for me. But I wouldn't wish to present the choice of the Kemetic (ancient Egyptian) religion as a negative one. Someone viewing the altar of Hathor in my bedroom asked *what's wrong with Buddha?* I'm not sure that anything's wrong with Buddha, but the Buddhist path does not feel to be one that I have been called to tread. I found myself drawn to (called by?) the ancient deities of Egypt long before I knew anything much about them. I knew a quite a lot about the deities for a long time before their religion started to make sense for me. It took the acquisition of a certain maturity before I was able to understand that a myth can be true – but not true in the sense that the laws of physics are true – or that accounts of past events are true. (Indeed, accounts of past events are not true in the sense that the laws of physics are true – there are many kinds of truth.)

My first encounter with the Kemetic deities came when I was perhaps eight or nine years old. I was certainly of junior school age. An old lady who lived up the road presented me with a stack of issues of a part work published in the 1920s and entitled *Wonders of the Past*. Or at least I have, over the years, thought of her as being an old lady who lived up the road. Thinking carefully now, I am not sure who she was. Indeed, looking back, this event – which was to have a profound effect on my life and my thinking – is surrounded with mystery. Who was my benefactress? I can't recall seeing her before or since the presentation of her gift. Why did she select me as the recipient of the gift rather than one of my siblings – or another child on the street? Looking back on this, more than half a century later, it takes on a supernatural air. Could the old lady have been a goddess? Perhaps she was one of the seven Hathors, presenting me with part of my fate.

Amongst the articles in *Wonders of the Past* was one entitled *The Gods of Ancient Egypt* by W M Flinders Petrie.

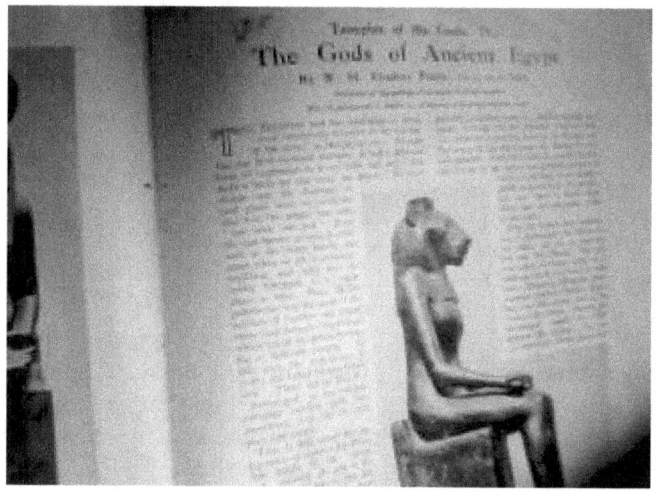

That, I suppose, was my first introduction to Kemetic religion. This article has been in my possession for most of my life, but I've never actually read it. My failure to read it is, I feel sure, no loss. I don't think that even Professor Petrie's greatest admirer would claim that he was an ideal choice to write on that subject. He was a good surveyor – and made the first accurate modern survey of the pyramid field at Giza. (I include the word *modern* in the last sentence as it is clear that the area must have been accurately surveyed before and during the construction of the pyramids.) Professor Petrie was also a fine deductive archaeologist whose achievements included devising the sequence dating method for prehistoric Egyptian pottery. This sequence dating incorporates the principle that features pass from function to decoration, but not vice versa. Pots with serviceable handles that incorporate indentations for the fingers are, therefore, earlier than ones in which this feature has turned into what seems to be a purely decorative wavy line.

Turning from Professor Petrie's strengths to his weaknesses… His talents did not include an ability to comprehend, interpret or comment upon belief systems at odds with the curious mixture of Christianity and science that passed for English thought in Victorian times.

While I have not read the article, I have read the captions to the illustrations – and they do not inspire much confidence. I think in particular of photographs of three goddess statues.

The caption tells us that they represent Isis, the Egyptian moon goddess. There is, for a start, no reason to regard Isis as a moon goddess. In fact, there is no evidence of any moon goddess from pharoaonic Egypt. My guess is that the confusion arises from the statues being crowned with a disc. Perhaps Professor Petrie considered that this must be either the sun or the moon. Hellenic mythology has a sun god and moon goddess – Egyptian mythology, too, has a sun god – therefore the disc on the head of the goddess must be the moon. If that is how Professor Petrie reasoned, he was in error. The disc crowning these goddess statues was most certainly the sun. Moreover, at least one of the statues is clearly not Isis – the photograph is sufficiently good to read the name of Hat-hor on the base. A second statue is unlike any image of Isis of which I am aware and almost certainly also represents Hat-hor. The third one could possibly be of Isis, but it is more likely to be yet another Hat-hor statue.

There is something paradoxical in an article I never read having much influence upon me. The misleadingly captioned pictures render it even more paradoxical. The major part of the influence came, no doubt, from the pictures themselves – my introduction to Kemetic iconography. Immediately, from first viewing, the images seemed neither alien nor bizarre. They not only felt familiar, but had a certain rightness. It was as though I had come home – or, at least, taken the first step on my homeward path.

Some features of the religion were immediately apparent from the images. One such feature is the clear conception of multiple deities. I can now conceive, in a theoretical way, that everything may be – ultimately – one. That you, me, my cat, the goddess Hat-hor, everything in the universe *may* all be aspects of one all-spirit. However, if this is so – that we are all one in a single being – then such an all-encompassing, and overriding, entity is ultimately unknowable and (in human terms) quite inconceivable. To predicate *anything* to that all-spirit would be blasphemous. (I suppose that predicating things to an all-spirit is exactly what such religions as Christianity and Islam are about.) Such is my mature view. As a child, I could not form such a conception in even a theoretical way. A multiplicity of deities, each of conceivable scope, made a great deal more sense.

A second point visible in the illustrations was the presence of both female and male deities. This agreed very well with what I knew of the world. The natural world – which is (surely) the same as, or some kind of reflection of, the divine world – is divided into female and male. One doesn't have to live very long in this world to observe that much. The concept of a single male deity presented by Christianity as I understood it didn't make sense.

Predictably, a further point to strike me was the animal or animal-headed forms presented by Kemetic iconography. These accorded well with a sense I already had of divinity within animals. I suppose I had conceived the idea that divinity resided in the natural order – although I might not have articulated it. Of all the creatures on the earth, we are the least natural. If nature is divinity, we must be, by that token, the least divine creatures. I suppose that this is the reason Christians are anxious to distance the deity from nature – but this is one of the aspects of Christianity that has never made sense to me. I may not always have formulated the feeling clearly, but it has been my continuing conviction that such divinity as we have is a function of what we have in common with the rest of the animal kingdom – not what separates us from it. Certainly, as a child, I had yet to conceive such ideas with any clarity – but I had a deep love of and respect for animals. From the start, the presence of animal forms in divine iconography felt right.

I think, here, of a tarot card – the nine of swords, named *Cruelty*. When I painted my pack, I depicted the nine of swords as a scene of cruelty involving a man (standing for the suit of Swords) and an elephant (standing for the number Nine). Eight of the swords have been thrust deep into the elephant's bleeding wounds. The elephant, for its part, has impaled the man's arm on a tusk and has lifted him off the ground. The man has the ninth sword in his free hand and is preparing to strike another futile blow.

The point of the card is not to do with blood-lust – it is to do with the frequently met human inability to let go. Where an animal would break off the conflict and depart, or at least attempt to depart, we all too often continue to strike blows. It is an essentially intellectual card: nature is often bloody, but not truly cruel. Cruelty encompasses a range of human behaviour that has to do with establishing and abusing power. It embraces playing politics (the establishment of power over our fellows) and (as an extreme example of the abuse of that power) the setting up of death camps. No other member of the animal kingdom indulges in such abominations. There is an irony in the way in which we call people *animals* for doing things that only a human being would do.

It seems to me that the low regard given to animals – and our animal selves – is part of a more general low value placed on the physical. There is a sense that, in some way, spirituality is better than physicality. This is the subject of Dory Previn's fine song *Mythical Kings and Iguanas* which puts it much better that I have. The point is encapsulated in the couplet:

Cry for the soul that will not face
The body as an equal place

I am uncomfortably aware that there is a paradox in my endorsement of that point of view. My main remit, in writing this, is to examine ideas and spiritual issues. Perhaps I should, instead, be writing about sex, dinner and other such important physical matters. In my defence, it seems to me that Kemetic religion assigns more importance to the physical than do most belief systems – and the aspects of the physical to which it assigns importance include dinner and, most certainly, sex.

Sex is so central to Kemetic religion that it needs to be addressed as a separate topic. The importance of food and drink is emphasised by the frequency with which the Egyptians used them (or their depictions) as religious offerings.

Also on the subject of physicality, it occurs to me that tenuous things can be physically important. The more solid and touchable something is, the shorter time we can manage without it. A healthy person can, I believe, survive several weeks without food (solids). The length of time we can survive without liquids is much shorter. Without air, we can live for only a few minutes. Exposure to the total absence of heat (absolute zero temperatures) is as near to instant death as we can measure. We cannot conclude that, because we are unable to grasp something physically, it is not physically important.

The Egyptian (Kemetic) pantheon and religion

Like men, the gods die, but they are not dead. Their existence – and all existence – is not an unchanging endlessness, but rather constant renewal.
– Erik Hornung *Conceptions of God in Ancient Egypt*

So – since junior school days – I have found the goddesses and gods of ancient Egypt particularly appealing. No doubt there are a number of reasons for this attraction – quite apart from the things I have already considered. One aspect is the complexity of Kemetic deities. People have asked me *what is Hat-hor the goddess of?* If she were, for example, an Hellenic goddess I would probably be able to give a short meaningful answer (albeit necessarily an incomplete one).
Question: *What is Aphrodite the goddess of?* **Answer:** *Love.*

By and large with the Egyptian deities, and certainly in the case of Hathor, such an answer would be more misleading than helpful. The complexity, for me, reflects the way the world is – and the nature of divinity in that world. If there are easy answers, they are (in my experience) frequently not worth having. Intricacy also means that one can relate to a deity and never fathom all that is there. One can know a person for years and still be surprised by them. If this is true of a person, how much more true should it be of a divinity? There is, too, the matter of mystery. In the end, the world – and divinity within it – is inevitably a mystery which we can never fathom. I see in the Egyptian deities, and their complexity, a celebration of this mystery.

This is a real religion, a faith that endured and satisfied many people throughout a long period. The world of late antiquity turned its back on the old traditions. Thereafter, these religious forms were forgotten or misrepresented – or both. The Victorians made great strides towards re-discovering such modes of viewing the world, only to place them in a cabinet of curiosities. It feels to me time – and past time – that old time religion was brought out of the cabinet and treated with the reverence it deserves.

Unlike later religions, the Kemetic faith is not a religion of the Book. There is no holy text, no word of God to hold us inflexibly. There are, of course, religious texts. Without these, we would not know enough of the Kemetic beliefs to regard them as forming a comprehensible religion. The point is that the texts make no claim – and never did claim – the status of such books as the Bible and the Koran. The Kemetic texts are in the service of religion, rather than the religion in the service of the texts. An important point, here, is that deities may create birds, beasts, plants, mountains, seas and stars – but they do not create books. Books are written by people – and people are fallible. If it comes to that, I am by no means certain that deities cannot be fallible. Even if a text were the work of a deity, that would not place it beyond all question. That, no doubt, is a key factor in Kemetic religion sitting (surprisingly?) comfortably with rationalism.

It is also a religion that acknowledges and honours femininity within the divine order. It acknowledges the importance of sexuality in creation, and interprets divine creation as an essentially sexual act. My feeling is that the low status accorded to sexuality in Christianity (and, no doubt, in other religions too) serves to foster misogyny. If there is no place for sexuality in the divine, there is no place for two sexes in divinity. As religious texts are mostly written by men (or, certainly, have largely been written by men historically) they take maleness as a default. The divine, for this reason, is presented as a male preserve. From that proceeds the idea that holiness resides in maleness – but not in femaleness. Religions with an exclusively male clergy (and an exclusively male viewpoint) follow naturally from this. Kemetic religion, by contrast, encourages a respect for sexuality – and cannot be properly celebrated without honouring the female.

Deities – and the world in general – are not constant or unchanging. They are renewed, and the process of renewal is essentially sexual – and requires both sexes. Not to change is not to exist. Not to have sexual processes is not to exist.

Those are plain literal truths, but – for the most part – the truths that this religion yields can be viewed either as poetic, or as one set of values in a system of multi-valued logic. They do not pretend to the coarse overly literal status fundamentalists claim for the books of more modern religions. For example, the sky is sometimes represented as a sacred cow with the stars along her belly. This does not tell us anything about astronomy, nor should we seek astronomical truth in the image. It may tell us something, however, about the way divinity is in the universe. Contemplating the image, seeking the outermost parts of its meaning, can reveal something of godhood: gems the grasping of which call for patient work.

The sky provides a handy example of the way in which the truths of Kemetic religion cannot be understood other than as poetic – or each as one set of values in a system of multi-valued logic. (How different those possibilities are is a matter open to question.) According to one myth, the sky is Hat-hor in the form of a cow with the stars along her belly. Another myth views the sky as another goddess, Nut, in the form of a woman arched over the earth. She swallows the sun in the evening and gives birth to the sun in the morning. A third myth depicts Nut as a sow who gives birth to her piglets (the stars) in the evening and devours them in the morning. Nor is the myth that the sun passes through Nut's body the only one to do with the sun by night. Another myth depicts the sun as making a perilous journey through the underworld, subject to attack by the serpent Apophis. We cannot construe this underworld as being the same place as the interior of Nut.

Conventional – single valued – logic would preclude holding as true all of these views (of the sky, and of the sun by night). It is an axiom of single valued logic that, if two assertions are contradictory, they cannot both be true. A system of multi-valued logic can assign separate values to each of several sets of assertions, so that they can co-exist. Adding more sets of values presents no problem – so the values proper to mythology and science can also co-exist. The values assigned to myths may or may not be regarded as *poetic*. It depends on how we define poetic truth.

At all events, the question of whether or not these things are true (in whatever sense) is an important one. Truth is sacred, and must be respected. It is, for example, no argument in favour of a belief that it is socially (or otherwise) useful for people to believe it. Upholding what we know to be false, for however fine-seeming reasons, is a form of holding that the end justifies the means. This is a road into the abyss.

Poetic Truth and Multi-Valued Logic

So – what is poetic truth? Is this an example?

My love is like a red, red rose
That's newly sprung in June
My love is like a melody
That's sweetly played in tune.

Robert Burns: *A Red, Red Rose*

It isn't easy to take this as literal truth. Mr Burns' *love* was, I assume,
either an emotion or a female member of the species homo sapiens. If the
former, it was a mental event – which surely does not resemble a physical
object such as *a red, red rose*. If his love was a woman, she would have
resembled a rose (*red, red* or otherwise) in being not only a physical
object, but also a living thing. However, roses and women are not very
similar – belonging to separate kingdoms of the living world (plant and
animal respectively). From the point of view of literal truth, he would
surely have been more nearly correct had he written:

My love is like a wild wart hog

A wart hog is, after all, not only a member of the animal kingdom but a
mammal – getting pretty close to human considered in the context of all
of creation. Of course, my wart hog line – while it may be closer to
literal truth – actually conveys the reverse of what Mr Burns intended. It
is evident that he wished to convey something of the beauty and delicacy
of his *love* – qualities for which the wart hog is not usually celebrated.

It would be easy to dismiss *A Red, Red Rose* as the sort of soupy thing
that girls like. (Although real girls, in my experience, are a lot less soupy
than some might suppose – the acceptability of the sentiments would very
much depend on who was uttering them!) It is, I suppose, in essence a
simile – and, as such, may need no special pleading as poetic truth.

Something rather different seems to be going on in this:

Hail to thee, blithe spirit!
Bird thou never wert –
That from heaven or near it
Pourest thy full heart
In profuse strains of unpremeditated art.

Percy Bysshe Shelley: *Ode to a Skylark*

Bird thou never wert? Taken as a literal assertion, a bird is exactly what a skylark wert, is and will continue to be. This does not seem to be susceptible to an explanation in terms of metaphor or simile. Nor can I believe that Mr Shelley was ignorant as to which class of creature a skylark belongs. If there is a way in which a skylark is not a bird, this is considerably closer to multi-valued logic. The idea seems to pre-suppose at least two distinct sets of assertions (separate realms of discourse) – biological, in which a skylark is a bird; and poetic, in which a skylark may not be a bird. Indeed, there very probably exists a poem in which a skylark is cited as being bird. If so – in poetic discourse – a skylark both is and is not a bird.

A possible construction upon Mr Shelley's words is that the skylark represents divinity at work in the world, rather than being no more than a creature in its own right (a bird). (In an earlier version of this text, I wrote *its just being a creature* – but this seemed to me to under-value animals, and I've attempted to reword the sentence. I continue to feel dissatisfied.)

If divinity at work in the world were to be taken as the sense of the stanza, the poetic truth it represents comes very close to myth.

For some people, mythology is much the same as poetic truth, for others it is not. I am not sure that the question of whether it is or is not poetic truth really makes much difference to anything of consequence. If not poetic as such, myth has in common with poetic truth that it lies in a separate realm of discourse from literal or everyday truth. Like poetic truth, contradictory assertions can each be true in their own contexts.

In fact, I think that contradictory assertions can each be true in their own contexts, even in the realm of literal truth. Take the following example:

When the sun rose yesterday, the sky was a vivid blue. As the sun climbed higher, it revealed banks of peach-coloured cloud.

It is a literal description of something I'd seen yesterday, when first composing this part of the text. (I did not cite that day's dawn because it was grey and a lot less interesting – were I departing from literal truth, I would probably have written *today* rather than *yesterday*.) From a scientific point of view, however, I have misstated what I observed. The sun did not rise; the celestial movement I observed was of the earth, rather than the sun. Literal truth for science is not always (or even usually?) the same as literal truth for ordinary discourse. Truth of all kinds is relative, complex and multi-layered. Whether we recognise it or not, we commonly work with multi-valued logic – as when we see the sun rise, although we know that what we perceive is the earth moving.

That much established, we may return to the divine realm of discourse, aware that its truths are not necessarily the same as (or readily compatible with) those of such other realms as the everyday, science or poetry. We will be aware, too, of this failing to render the truths any less valid.

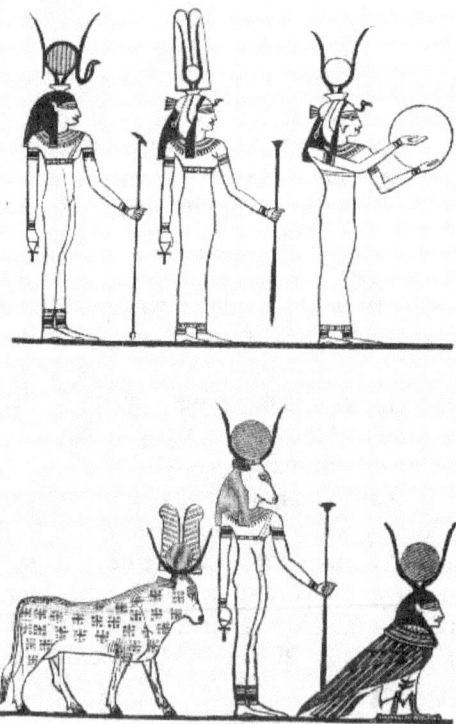

Hat-hor

Hathor was so widely loved that she was present everywhere Egyptians were found.
Barbara S. Lesko – *The Great Goddesses of Egypt* p97

I regard myself as a Kemetic Rationalist – but, more precisely, I am a devotee of Hat-hor.

Hat-hor was a popular goddess worshipped, in ancient times, by both sexes. While that is so, she seems to have been especially popular with women. Amongst the votive objects they left at her shrines are beautiful pieces of decorative fabric. In ancient times, as now, the production of decorative fabrics was more associated with women than men. Beyond this, Geraldine Pinch observes:

Some of the textiles from Deir el-Bahri apparently show groups of unrelated women. The high proportion of female donors on stelae [stone slabs similar in appearance to modern grave stones – PFJ]... has been emphasised... Two of the intermediary texts at Deir el-Bahri are addressed chiefly to women, as is a text on a similar statue from the temple of Mehyt at Thinis. It could be argued that the women shown on the stelae and textiles are all priestesses of Hathor, but while appeals to the living inscribed on temple statues often specifically address priests, the intermediary texts at Deir el-Bahri refer not to priestesses but to 'young girls' or to 'noble ladies as well as poor girls'. The Thinis statue simply addresses the women of the town of Pi-Mehyt. This indicates that women of all kinds were expected to visit these temples, not just those who served the goddess on a regular basis.

– Geraldine Pinch: *Votive Offerings to Hathor*. Griffith Institute, 1993 pp342-343.

This seems to me clear evidence that, in ancient times, the cult of Hat-hor appealed strongly to women and girls.

The origins of Hat-hor's worship vanish into the mists of early history, but are perhaps not of the essence. Rather, I note with pleasure that when the goddess steps out clearly for the first time, in the age of the pyramids, she does so in a magnificent manner. Her image emerged in a series of the finest statues ever carved. The sculptures represent triads of Hat-hor, King Men-Kau-Re, and in each case a local divinity from a place associated with the Hat-hor cult.

The beautiful figures appear from a smooth surface representing the primal waters the Egyptians conceptualised as Naunet (female – goddess of the primal waters) and Nun (male). The King strides purposefully, but the goddesses are at rest – and strike me as more powerful for being so. The primal waters continue, and continue to bear fruit, in the amniotic fluid contained within the female. It is a statement specifically of Hathor's power and majesty, but has much to say of female power and divinity in general.

Hat-hor could have originally been a sky goddess with strong associations with fertility. Her name means Mansion of Horus (the *us* is a termination added by the Hellenes). That is to say the enclosure of the sacred falcon. The hieroglyph that forms her name (the one visible on a supposed image of Isis in Professor Petrie's article in *Wonders of the Past*) is of the sacred falcon in an enclosure. If one imagines a clear blue sky in which a falcon circles, one will surely be close to the significance of her name. The name is, itself, poetry. Her aspect as a sky goddess is emphasised in her title Mistress of Heaven.

The Hat-hor hieroglyph – of the enclosed falcon – has sexual reference, obvious once one has seen it. The idea came to me in contemplating the hieroglyph during my devotions. The falcon (Horus) is the penis and the enclosure (Hat-hor) the vagina. Alternatively, the falcon (Horus) is the fetus and the enclosure (Hat-hor) the womb. The alternatives are the sexual act and its consequent (divine) creation.

When one first sees the hieroglyph, inevitably, the falcon forms the foreground and the framing enclosure the background. During my devotions, looking at the divine name, I deliberately reverse this – focusing on the enclosure rather than the enclosed.

The process is akin to looking at one of the double images so beloved of gestalt theorists – switching, for example, between the two faces and the vase:

…or between the young and old women:

In making this shift, I hope to focus upon the all too often overlooked female aspect of deity.

It occurs to me that the Hat-hor hieroglyph is, essentially, a falcon in a box. One of the senses of *box* is a slang term for the female genitals.

Hat-hor is associated with (amongst other things) erotic love, intoxication, music and dance. She is a patroness of women in childbirth, and of children. Indeed, she goes beyond being a patroness of women in childbirth – every woman actually becomes Hat-hor at the moment of giving birth. Hat-hor is the female creator. The seven Hat-hors (each an aspect of Hat-hor) are present at each birth and are (in some ways) akin to the Hellenic Fates.

The goddess has strong associations with healing, and her temple at Dendera – her chief cult centre – included a sanatorium.

She also has a terrible face. *The Book the Cow of Heaven* relates a myth in which Ra, the sun god, ordered the destruction of the human race. It was Hat-hor who performed the slaughter. Nor would she relent when the sun god changed his mind. So he commanded that the earth be covered with a mixture of beer and red dye. Hat-hor took the red beer for blood, drank it and became intoxicated. When she awoke, the blood-lust had passed. I think it is important to distinguish between this blood-lust, which lies within the nature of Hat-hor, and calculated cruelty, which does not. My remarks on the tarot card, nine of swords, once more have bearing here. Nature is often bloody, but not truly cruel. The Nazis (for example) were cruel, as are those who abuse children. Hat-hor – like a predator (I think, for example, of a fox in a chicken coop) – may be subject to blood-lust, but not to cruelty.

I am aware that the common idea of foxes' blood-lust in chicken coops is based upon faulty observation. It is true that the fox will kill (or attempt to kill) every chicken in the coop – and will usually leave most of the corpses. But the fox will take all of the corpses, burying them for future consumption, if the animal is not disturbed.

Just as the fox's blood-lust is based on faulty observation, so may that of the goddess. The motivations of deities are more difficult to fathom than those of animals. With the caveat that the fox's blood-lust is not what we think it is, the analogy may be allowed to stand. Doubtless the goddess' rage is also different from the way it may seem.

The myth of Hat-hor's destruction of mankind (as narrated in *The Book the Cow of Heaven*) is sometimes compared with the Noah myth. A difference between the two – that strikes me as important – is that in the

Noah myth destruction is more indiscriminate. In both myths, the gods are enraged by the actions of humanity. In *The Book the Cow of Heaven*, the wrath is firmly directed at our species. By contrast, Noah's flood also drowns large numbers of unoffending creatures. Only a pair of each species is saved, with the clear implication that the survival of individual animals is of no account, only the survival of the species matters.

We see Hat-hor more usually in her nurturing role – but she who can nurture can also destroy. There are important lessons in this – and life should show us that creating the new goes hand in hand with destroying the old. The healer is a destroyer, although the destroyer is not necessarily a healer.

Hat-hor is also the deity whom the Egyptians most often associated with foreign countries. We all, I suppose, live under the Mistress of Heaven. I see this aspect of Hat-hor as especially fitting her for worship in a foreign place and a foreign time. That said, her associations with erotic love, intoxication, music and dance are also ubiquitous. If every woman becomes Hat-hor at the moment of giving birth – and the seven Hat-hors attend each child – these too are matters that remain unaltered and that engage every country.

The association of erotic love, intoxication, music and dance in Hat-hor is noteworthy. If we consider the lives of musicians, for example, how often are their weaknesses to be found in erotic love and/or intoxication? Such names as Billie Holiday and Janis Joplin come instantly to mind in this context.

The mention of Hat-hor's association with erotic love brings us to the central place assigned to sex in Kemetic religion.

Sex and the single goddess

Kemetic religion includes perhaps the most explicitly sexual of all
creation myths. Stated simply, it is that Atum performed the first act of
creation by masturbating. As an allusion to this, Hat-hor is regarded as
the hand of Atum.

The myth makes a lot of sense. Given that divine creation is sexual (and
a look at the world should assure us that this is so) how could the first act
of creation have taken place? The myth, then, affirms the central place of
sex in the creative process – and in the divine order. Atum may be
regarded as the original undifferentiated godhead. Within this first deity
are the potentiality of both the female (Hat-hor as the hand) and the male
(the penis of Atum).

Back in the days when I would have liked to have believed in the
Kemetic faith – but found myself unable to do so – the sexual aspects of
the religion were not easy to discover. An example that seems to typify
the (in this case literal) cover up dates to the mid 1960s. I visited what
was then known as University College Department of Egyptology
Museum – now called the Petrie Museum. (Named after the Professor
Petrie whose article on the gods of ancient Egypt I'd seen in *Wonders of
the Past*, when I was a child.) One of the more impressive objects in the
museum is a large relief sculpture of a king dancing before the god Min.
The god is represented as having an erect penis. When I saw the stones, a
notice (explaining what the carving depicted) covered this detail, if *detail*
is the correct word.

Back in the 1960s, my chief source on sex in ancient Egypt was an article
on *Sexual Behaviour* by Jean Yoyotte. It occupies less than a page in *A
Dictionary of Egyptian Civilization* edited by George Posener and
published by Methuen in 1962. In addition to the *Sexual Behaviour*
article, page 260 also contains the end of a piece about King *Seti I* and the
start of an article on *Sheep*. That said, it was better than nothing.
Monsieur Yoyotte's remarks begin with this:

*There is no study yet available of the ancient Egyptians' attitude towards
sex or of their ideas about physical intercourse.*

They end with this:

*In a country of educated people there were still some who scribbled
indescribable pictures on ostraca. Propriety has prevented the Turin*

*Museum from exhibiting the famous papyrus in which the capers of a
bald priest and a Theban coquette are depicted in a coarse manner and
annotated with ribald remarks.*

(Ostraca – the singular is ostracon – are fragments of limestone or broken
pottery inscribed in ink. They were the ancient Egyptian equivalent to
cheap paper. Papyrus was expensive. Surviving ostraca include such
things as laundry lists, and documents relating to the hire of donkeys.)

I relied on Jean Yoyotte's article during a time when I was taking an
especially active interest in ancient Egypt – visiting museums and buying
quite a lot of books on the subject. With tougher times in the 1970s – and
very often little disposable income – I lost touch with current Egyptology.
During the second half of the 1990s, for perhaps the first time in about a
quarter of a century, I entered a bookshop with a good stock of recent
Egyptological work. A glance at some of the book titles revealed that
much had changed whilst I had not been paying attention.

There were now a number of books on the subject of women in ancient
Egypt – a topic that had been neglected in the 1960s. (In those days, my
best source on the subject was half a chapter in book mostly concerned
with women in ancient Hellas.) A glance at the authors' names revealed
that the shift mirrored a change in Egyptology – it was clearly a lot less
male-dominated than it had been.

Lise Manniche, one of the rising generation of female Egyptologists, had
written a book entitled *Sexual Life in Ancient Egypt* (details will be found
in the bibliography). She reproduced some of what Jean Yoyotte termed
indescribable pictures on ostraca. Predictably, they turn out to be fairly
easy to describe.

Propriety had not prevented Ms Manniche from reproducing the pictures
included in the Turin erotic papyrus – nor from translating the
fragmentary writing it bears (Monsieur Yoyotte's *ribald remarks*, or so I
assume). Perhaps the most ribald is this exchange:

(She:) 'Leave my bed alone, and I'll...semen(?) at me(?).'
(He:) 'My big phallus... which suffers...inside.'

(Sexual Life in Ancient Egypt p110.)

The pictures are not always a great deal easier to follow than the
fragmentary text – although their general import is plain enough. I was

especially interested to see that the scenes seem to include pony girls (pulling a chariot). Previously, I'd been unaware of such a depiction before the mid-twentieth century. Many things go back further than one might imagine. Lise Manniche has this to say of the pictures:

It has been suggested that the pictures represent the amorous adventures of a priest of Amun and a Theban whore, or that they were intended as an imitation of events at a higher level, in the world of the gods. Some have attempted to identify the chief male character as the king in whose reign the scroll was written.
(*Sexual Life in Ancient Egypt* p107.)

Another book – *Sacred Sexuality in Ancient Egypt* by Ruth Schumann Antelme and Stephane Rossini (Inner Traditions, 2001) also suggests that the Turin erotic papyrus may be – at least partially – religious.

This book concludes:

Hathor's secrets are numerous, varied, and often strange, but all derive from the first becoming, the divine creation of the universe, and commingle, on the terrestrial level, with humanity's history since its inception. Hathor the Golden One, the Sovereign of Love, and Lady of Death, Mistress of Drunkenness, the ravaging Distant One and the tender Bastet, joyous Mistress of music and dance, the generous Celestial Cow, lady of the Vulva and womb of the world, Ra's burning eye, his untameable daughter, Uraeus who defends her father and protects the king, the Unique One who is always everywhere and nowhere, as ungraspable as love.
Sacred Sexuality in Ancient Egypt p162.

Such is she whom I worship.

31

Innocent of the Omni-s

The omnivore has eaten my omni-lette

I had been corresponding (on religious matters) with a friend for a long while before he remarked, in evident surprise, that I didn't see Hat-hor as all-powerful. This seemed so obvious to me that I had not previously bothered to mention it.

When I came to think about the matter, it seemed to me that this was probably the key difference between polytheistic religions and monotheism. While my devotions are directed solely to Hat-hor, I view my religion as polytheistic. My assumption is that she is one amongst many deities.

Monotheism – as I understand it – defines its single deity in terms of three omni-s: omnipotence, omniscience and omnipresence. The god (and it never seems to be a goddess!) is viewed as all powerful, all knowing and present in every place.

The polytheistic definition of a deity is necessarily different – it would simply not make sense to predicate the three omni-s to more than one deity. If more than one deity occupied the same space (= all space) and knew exactly the same things (= all things) surely they would be the same entity. I (the writer) am a different person from you (the reader) because we do not occupy the same space at the same time – and because our heads are full of different things. As to omnipotence – imagine two omnipotent deities attempting to do conflicting things. They couldn't both succeed – so they couldn't both be omnipotent.

Myths from many cultures, including that of Egypt, show the deities as being less than all-powerful. To cite an example, I return to the myth of Hat-hor and the destruction of mankind. Ra, the sun god, has dispatched Hat-hor to destroy our rebellious species. When Ra relents, Hat-hor is unwilling to stop the slaughter. So – Ra has a great quantity of beer dyed with red ochre and covers the land with this. Believing that she is wading in blood, Hat-hor pauses to lap the beer. She falls into a drunken stupor and – when she awakes – forgets to continue the slaughter. That Hat-hor fails to destroy our entire species shows her not to be omnipotent. Her failure to recognize the dyed beer for what is shows her not to be omniscient. Likewise, her lack of knowledge on this implies that she was not about when the red ochre was mixed with the beer – and that excludes omnipresence.

An examination of other myths, from many cultures, will show the same implications about multiple deities. This is perhaps most clearly seen in the very widespread myths about conflict between the gods. In Kemetic myth, we have the contending of Horus and Seth. In Nordic mythology, Baldur contends with Loki. Other examples may occur to the reader.

One of the more odd features of monotheistic religions is that they fail to take this on board properly. Christian myth, indeed, includes divine conflict – in the form of the rebellion of Satan. How could Satan plot a rebellion against a deity who was present when the plot was hatched (omnipresence) and who knew all about it from the start (omniscience)? And what would be the point in plotting against an omnipotent entity? How could the omnipotent one fail to be victorious? The idea is more extreme than a boxing bout that matched the heavyweight champion of the world against a new born babe.

The three omni-s seem to make a nonsense of many things – not just myth patterns. Why should a devotee pray to tell an omniscient deity about things that she or he must already (by definition) know?

There is, of course, a big disparity between Hat-hor and me – but that disparity is infinitely less than that between a Christian and her or his conceived deity. I like this aspect of polytheism. An infinite disparity seems to me to take inequality too far. In my religious conceptions, Hat-hor has great but finite power and great but finite knowledge. Nor is Hat-hor present in every place – hence my devotions regularly including:

Thank you goddess – thank you for your presence in this place

This would make no sense were I to conceive the goddess as omnipresent. Rather than that, I think it possible for a place to be literally godforsaken.

For me, the altar in my bedroom, and the divine images of the goddess, are of enormous importance – as places where Hat-hor is present. The images, indeed, form bodies for the goddess. Furthermore, an image of the goddess worn on a chain about the neck may help facilitate the presence of the goddess, whilst the devotee is away from the altar (where her other images dwell).

It is possible that the need for such an image, worn about the person, is transitory. For several years, I wore a golden goddess on a chain almost every time I left the house. (My feeling is that there must have been moments of abstraction in which I failed to fasten the chain about my neck.) Then, one morning, the image was not in her accustomed place – and (several years later) I haven't glimpsed her since. My best guess is that my cat was responsible for the disappearance, although there is no way for me to be certain. The cat is, after all, a sacred animal, and may have acted as an agent of the goddess. Perhaps the vanishment of the golden image on a chain signified that I no longer required her.

Catholics seem to do something similar in wearing crucifixes about their necks – which I find puzzling. (My impression, going a little further, is that they don't regard the need for crucifixes as transitory.) If the deity is omnipresent, why is it considered efficacious to do this? Is this just another example of failing properly to think monotheism through? And why is the deity represented in his most disempowered form? Could this be to minimise the disparity between deity and devotee? Personally, if the goddess is to be with me, I would prefer her to be depicted in an empowered form. I would not, for example, wish to wear an image of the goddess in her drunken stupor.

Of course, it is possible for the goddess to be present without an image. (This, I suppose, is a reason that the need for an image about one's person may be a transitory requirement.) The goddess is clearly older than her oldest image. If she was the hand of Atum, Hat-hor was present at the moment of first creation – the moment (translated into the realm of myth) that scientists know as the big bang. She is also present, for example, in music and in giving birth. Those two instances are of her passing presence in places where she may not always reside. In presenting Hat-hor with an image that pleases her – and in which she is willing to reside – her presence may be granted in a more ongoing way. But the need for such an image may pass.

Images

Images form an important element in Kemetic belief. The Egyptian word for *image* is *twt*, generally rendered into English as *tut*, and is the first element in the name of Tutankhamun… Tut-ankh-Amun, the living image of the (god) Amun. Images are central to Kemetic worship, in some wise forming bodies for deities to inhabit. We may worship a worthy imagine, dedicated to and accepted by a deity, because – in a real sense – it (she, he) *is* the deity.

My feeling is that, whether we acknowledge it or not, almost everybody senses the power of images. We experience it during childhood in seeking comfort from a teddy bear, or whatever soft toy fate or our parents allot to us.

Later in life, we may find that images in art galleries have the ability to release powerful emotions. The emotions are within us, but the images have the ability to trigger them. Insofar as the emotions felt by different viewers are substantially similar, the power to release emotion lies within the image. The artwork has become something more than we might expect an inanimate object to be. If the universe is alive, perhaps the distinction between the animate and inanimate is not quite as it seems at first glance.

I was intrigued, some years ago, to hear my brother and his wife speak of *protective creatures*. The reference was not to living animals, but to ceramic images of dragons, and the like. Placing one in the hallway, my brother seemed to think, was efficacious in protecting the entrance to his house. The concepts embodied in this overheard husband/wife conversation sit very easily with my outlook, but my brother and his wife regarded themselves as Quakers. I'm no expert on Quakerism, but feel sure that its tenets exclude the idea of images possessing the power to act as guardians of the home. Indeed, my feeling is that this would sit uneasily with any form of Christianity, or indeed any monotheistic religion. Possibly the sense of the power of images is in itself too powerful, to ubiquitous, to be denied by one's professed faith. Perhaps, if we scratch below the surface, few people fail to harbour ideas at odds with their religion (or denial of religion). At bottom, we may all take a Kemetic view, whether or not we acknowledge or articulate it.

If the universe is alive, it is scarcely surprising that presences – call them spirits, souls, *akhu*, or what one will – are to be encountered in images. But some presences strike us more forcibly than others. It is a commonplace that a work of art commands a greater presence than a mass produced item, and this suggests that the spirit of an image is something introduced by its creator. An alternative interpretation is that the qualities of the work of art attract a pre-existing spirit to inhabit it. Or it may be that the creative process, and the work produced from it, forms a gestalt. That the spirit we detect in the work has a oneness with the act of creation and the presence (a muse, perhaps) that inspired it. Pre-existence and arising from a process may not be irreconcilable.

My feeling, as a writer of fiction, is that spirits – whether pre-existing, arising from my creativity, or both – can and do inhabit the words I write. This, clearly, extends the idea of *image* beyond literal, visual, images. My experience is that, in my major work, characters assume life and – having done so – it is they rather than I who direct the work. An example is Fluff, a character who has survived several recastings of the text, and who plays a prominent part in my novel *Margaret Again*. Initially, I introduced Fluff as no more than a convenient figure to take the wet outerwear from the central characters, as they emerge from the rain into a house. Without thought on my part, or seemingly without it, she showed signs of character almost at once with this:

With a quick movement of her foot, the bondling slid a rug over a small puddle, drips from our waterproofs – Fluff didn't seem to have been chosen for dedication to housework.

Soon, Fluff's presence seemed to light up any passage in which she appeared. With surprise, a few chapters later, I found myself thinking *that turned into a Fluff chapter*.

In another novel (*Jane*), a character has this to say of Fluff:

"She was another Palace Victoria slave," Barguin settled herself on the couch. "I suppose her name meant people thought she was stupid, head full of fluff, and she could seem that way – but it was just an act. When you got to know her, you found that she was as bright as any of us. In fact, the better you knew her, the brighter she seemed – and in more ways than one. The first time you met her, there seemed nothing very remarkable about the girl. Then, when you began to know Fluff, she lit up the entire room. You couldn't help but love her."

Barguin's words closely reflect my own feelings on Fluff. (Although Barguin herself feels to me a living presence, by no means a mere cipher – and her character and views, in general, are not mine.)

Fluff is not an isolated instance – I've known many characters to assume life. Nor, I believe, is the experience exclusively mine. Having myself experienced the phenomenon, I discovered that other writers of fiction have reported what seems to be the same thing.

Books, like visual images, have a presence – and so do at least some of the characters within them. Having lived with books for much of my life, I sense that the volumes in my home affect the atmosphere of my living space. There have certainly been books with which I was relieved to part, and the passing of which seemed to improve my life. Examples include the works of the unlamented Mr. Crowley, which I am much pleased to have been absent from my shelves for many years.

On a rather different note, it seemed that the Bible didn't wish to be owned by me – I've possessed several copies, but they seemed unable, or unwilling, to remain with me. The last one I had was purchased in a Leicester junk shop. I chose it because it was an edition used by the school I'd attended twenty or twenty-five years before, and contained illustrations that stimulated me as a child. I was much astonished, on getting it home, to discover a stamp impression inside the front cover marking it as the property of the church (at a guess 130 or 140 miles away) favoured by my mother. Giving the book to my parents, for return to the church, I think I had finally done with the Bible – and, I hope, it had done with me.

Another example occurs to me of something that is not, in the usual sense, an image. A friend's mother planted a rose bush in memory of her late husband, and talks to the plant as though it were he. Her actions may not make sense in terms of whatever belief system she professes, but make perfect sense in Kemetic terms. It may be a further indication that, below the outer levels of belief, a Kemetic core is commonly found. If it is so found, I submit, that is not without cause.

For many people, I think, such creeds as Christianity are no more than wafer thin veneers covering things that, at root, they sense to be true.

Returning to images in a more literal sense, children's toys form an interesting example. I am struck by the gulf between brand new, pristine, mass-produced toys and those with which a child has played. There is to me, for example, something disturbing in the mass ranks of Barbie dolls in a large toy shop. I really would not like to be in such a shop late at night, after closing time. Such mass produced, unsullied, human images strike me as soulless, creepy. But, in the process of play, a doll – any doll – becomes something other.

Play, I think, is crucially important to a doll. Those abominations, collectors' dolls, seem to me far creepier than brand new pristine Barbies. The Barbie dolls have at least the potential for play. Collectors' dolls are simply monstrous.

I evoke such a doll in Chapter 2 of my novel *Margaret*:

After ripping away the wrappings, to my strong disappointment, I found myself looking at a doll. It wasn't even a pretty doll, in fact it was downright ugly. Nor was it the kind of doll with which a little girl could play. The thing represented a lady of fashion clothed in white lacy garments a child's touch would ruin in seconds.

Although this doll represents an adult, my feeling is that the many objects of the kind depicting children are even worse. (Perhaps I hesitated to write about one of those shuddersome things... books, as I have observed, are given lives of their own.)

The question may arise as to what extent the played-with toy is possessed by a pre-existing spirit, and to what extent the child creates the spirit through the act of play. Essentially, I think that question has no answer – and, like many questions that have no answer, it may be more a seeming-question than a real one.

Another question is whether a deity encountered in an image is of a piece with the spirit found in a well-loved toy, or are these entirely distinct from one another? The latter seems indicated by the way in which the same deity may be present in widely scattered images, whilst the familiar spirit of a toy seems to have a single home. Neither does a toy's spirit have the power, radiance and transcendence we see in a goddess or god. Yet both the toy and the embodiment of the deity may be examples of *akhu*, plural of the Egyptian word *akh*, effective spirits – at which we will take a brief look in a subsequent section. Books, fictitious characters – and memorial rose bushes, too – may all embody *akhu*.

Stepping to meet Hat-hor

More than forty years passed between my initial encounter with Hat-hor's name and my first devotions to the goddess. It was a long time. My first thought is that, for most of this period, I was not so much stepping to meet Hat-hor as dawdling on the way. Perhaps, though, I am being unfair to myself – I had a lot of work to do, a lot of assumptions to shed, before I could hope to meet the goddess.

As I've said, I was perhaps eight or nine years old when an elderly lady presented me with a stack of issues of a part work published in the 1920s and entitled *Wonders of the Past*. Amongst the articles it contained was one by Margaret Murray on the temples of Hat-hor at Dendera and Horus at Edfu. I was familiar with at least the name and iconography of the goddess whilst still at junior school. Interesting, too, that the article was the work of one of the few female Egyptologists of her day.

Margaret Murray was to re-emerge for me when I finally decided to do some reading on ancient Egypt. On one of my teenage birthdays (possibly my 16th) someone gave me a book token. I spent it on the three British mass market paperbacks, available at that time, on the subject of my favourite ancient culture. One of the three was the Four Square edition of Margaret Murray's *The Splendour That Was Egypt*. One of the text figures in the book was the hieroglyph that forms Hat-hor's name – the first time this had been drawn to my attention.

In the meantime, my religious affiliation had been subject to change. I'm not sure exactly what religion I favoured as a child. I certainly found the Kemetic deities attractive, and equally certainly was not impressed by Christianity. Part of my trouble with Christianity was that I saw it as part of the respectability that was so important to my parents – and that I loathed and despised. Another trouble was the association between Christianity and my attendance at Sunday school – something that I deeply resented. I was not pleased to attend school Monday to Friday, and would have much preferred to spend my time in the woods. Having my Sunday spoilt as well was something I regarded with impotent rage. My rage was impotent because bunking off Sunday school was not a realistic option. We were supplied with books into which stamps were stuck. Each week we were given a stamp which we were expected (dutifully) to stick in its proper place. The Sunday school stamps were, of course, the check on whether we were really attending. I hated the stamp book as much as I hated Sunday school itself. The Sunday school I attended was attached to a church a bus ride distant from my home (the church to which belonged the Bible purchased many years later in Leicester). The nearest church was too low church, insufficiently respectable, for my mother. I recall, one week, waiting for the bus homewards with my rage at Sunday school and the stamp book welling to bursting point. I started to shred the stamp book with my teeth. A woman in the bus queue said something about a child being so hungry.

When I was taken to church, I was simply bored and drifted off into a stupor. I recall being repeatedly aroused from my dazed condition by the creed. My attention was caught by:

He suffered under Pontius Pilate

Which I misheard as:

He suffered under Pontius Pirate

I approved of pirates for much the same set of reasons as I disapproved of Christianity. I perceived them as free spirits – and most definitely not respectable. The word *suffered* connected well with pirates. The whole basis of piracy, as far as I understood it, was to make respectable people suffer. Make them walk the plank – or maroon them on desert islands – and jolly well serve them right. So, this seeming reference to a pirate (engaged in the proper business of that calling) had my sudden rapt attention. I listened carefully to the following passage – but, alas, there was nothing more about pirates. My conclusion was that I had missed most of the section on piracy. That being so, I made an effort to listen to the service from the start – but I couldn't manage it. Always, I drifted off into a stupor to be suddenly aroused by the mention of *Pontius Pirate*.

I did have a brief period of Christianity during my early teens. The confirmation classes held by Father Head, rector of St Clement's, Leigh-on-Sea, were sufficiently inspirational to provoke my brief adoption of the religion he espoused. (Though, that said, I was probably making of Christianity something with which Father Head would neither have agreed nor approved.) And this Christianity did prove no more than a passing phase.

Thereafter, for several years, my usual religious (or irreligious) stance was atheism. This anti-creed was tinged with a wish that I could believe in the Kemetic deities. But, at that time, my thought processes were too literal and too vulgar to sustain such a belief. For me, then, the belief would have entailed thinking that a rocket shot into space would collide with the body of a goddess. Well – come to think of it – maybe that is true in a sense, but not in the vulgarly literal sense my teenage self envisaged. I did devote some effort to trying to make sense of the Kemetic pantheon – drawing up an elaborate family tree, relating the deities of whom I was aware to the other goddesses and gods. Where I could discover no reference to relationships, I simply invented them. I was clearly moved by a desire to systematise the religion. There was an element in this that was true to the spirit of Kemetic religion – the idea that the relationships between deities are important. What my teenage self was unable to encompass was the fluidity and ambiguity of these relationships. In failing to encompass this, I had missed the heart of the religion.

My mid-teens atheism was of quite an extreme kind. I recall a fellow student at Southend-on-Sea Municipal College questioning my beliefs – I must have been about sixteen at the time. Having elicited that I didn't believe in a god, he asked whether I believed in Jesus. "No," I replied. When he asked me to clarify that I said that I didn't think that any such person had ever lived.

After my teens, I regarded myself variously as an atheist, a polytheist, a pagan, a Gnostic and (eventually) an agnostic. For quite a bit of this time the atheist bit was what I actually believed, and the polytheist stance what I would have liked to believe.

Seeing is not necessarily believing, as a strange experience demonstrates. It was the summer 1970, I was 24 years old. Although I did take psychedelic drugs in those days, I was not under the influence of any at the time of the experience. I was walking somewhere in the vicinity of Lancaster with a view of open, flat, countryside. I am now surprised not to know my location more precisely than that. As I looked over the flat ground stretching away to my right, I saw a great number of misty pillars of enormous height. A non-corporeal presence seemed to be with me, telling me that these were the gods. It told me that one of them was Isis and – as I looked – one of the misty pillars took on the form given to the goddess in Egyptian iconography. At that moment, I believed it – and was profoundly shaken by the experience. Within the day, however, and perhaps within the hour, I no longer believed it. I might have liked to have regarded it as a drug-induced experience – but was unable to do so. (Partly because I wasn't under the influence of drugs at the time – and partly because it was unlike any drug-induced experience I ever had.) Very quickly, I came to regard it as a psychotic incident – and (perhaps wisely) did not share my experience with anyone. Thinking about it now,

I don't what reality the experience had – and, indeed, don't think it matters. The point is that to see a goddess is not to believe in her – religious belief is of a different order from belief in physical objects. Religious belief is not a question of what one sees or doesn't see. It is a matter of how one interprets what one sees – and of how one relates to it.

I adopted the *pagan* label after discovering and joining the Pagan Movement. However, the British pagan scene proved not to be what I hoped and, after a while, I concluded that it wasn't for me. It centred (and probably still centres) on Celtic deities. Whilst these deities may be fine in their way, they are not my goddesses and gods – as I realised from the first. They felt alien to me, and still do.

The late unlamented Mr Crowley inspired the Gnostic business. In the early 1970s I discovered his writings and – for several years – he was a big influence on my thinking. I refer to Crowley as *unlamented* because he did a lot of harm to those who associated themselves with him. One can tell a lot more about people by looking at what they do (and not least how they treat others) than by considering what they say. With the passage of time, however, I have come to like what Crowley wrote a lot less than I once did. It now seems to me that (like the Satanists) he was essentially a Christian heretic.

One thing that appealed to me about Crowley was his naming his aeons after Kemetic deities (in sequence Isis, Osiris and Horus). That said, I am sure that Crowley's understanding of Kemetic religion was rudimentary – and rather crude. In line with the Gnosticism espoused by Crowley, I attempted to form my own religion from an eclectic mixture of faiths. On the plus side, this permitted me to incorporate Kemetic elements into my belief system. Alas, the result was neither coherent, convincing nor satisfying. The appeal of such an approach is now obscure as far as I'm concerned, but it seemed a good idea at the time.

As Crowley's influence upon me waned, I passed into a non-religious phase. Perhaps, during the years that followed, I might have described myself as an agnostic – if asked. I'm not sure that anyone did ask. In some ways, fantasy fiction took the place of religion during the earlier parts of this non-religious phase. To an extent, such fiction addresses some of the longings that religion answers – or attempts to answer. Amongst these, certainly, is the sense of mystery and wonder. In regard to fantasy fiction as a religious substitute, I note that the first attempts at fantasy in the modern sense belong to the age of reason. They emerged as religious belief was called into question.

I write *fantasy in the modern sense* because ancient myths and epics often have the look of fantasy fiction. (Or, more accurately, fantasy fiction may have the look of ancient myths and epics!) The difference is that, where fantasy fiction attempts to convey truths, they are not the same kind of truths as those that may be found in myths. They look more to our own nature than to the nature of deity.

Perhaps in parts of my agnostic period – and especially the later parts – sex took the place of religion. Although I did not realise it at the time, this was steering me back in the general direction of Kemetic belief – to which sex is central.

In the mid 1990s, I discovered a shop on Bury Place (near the British Museum) called the Egyptian Bazaar. The stock included some fine images of Kemetic deities – to which I felt drawn, but which, at the time, I begrudged the money to buy. Also in stock, were some small figures of baked clay molded in the ancient style. These were very cheap – and I bought two. One was an ushabti, the other a crude figure of a goddess. At the time of purchase, I thought the goddess figure depicted Isis nursing the infant Horus. Looking at it later, I wasn't sure. She could equally have been Hat-hor holding some kind of staff or sceptre. I placed the two figures on a shelf and, for quite a long time, left them there.

The ushabti figure I have still scarcely touched – but the goddess is another matter. My cat fell seriously ill, and I was doubtful whether he would survive the night (so that I could take him to the vet the following day). It was beyond my power to do anything for him – apart from what I did. I took the crude goddess figure, set her up on the desk beside my bed and – for the first time in many years – I prayed. Addressing her simply as *goddess*, I asked that she help my cat. Thereafter, although continuing to be ill, he started to recover. Afterwards, I thanked the goddess – and, with that, my prayers rested for two or three years.

Times of trouble brought me back to the goddess. The friend with whom I shared a house and I became objects for persecution by Forest Gate thugs. We had bricks through our front window on two occasions – and suffered a number of assaults. As a result of the worst incident, I suffered a broken arm and required stitches around my eye. We needed to move house – but the process of re-housing dragged on for almost a year.

While it had seemed fine to ask the goddess a favour on behalf of my cat – it seemed a lot less so to ask a favour on my own behalf – especially on so short an acquaintance. Attempting to form a relationship with the goddess was another matter – less presumptuous, and possibly overdue. The first step, I thought, was a better (and less ambiguous) goddess figure. So, I returned to the shop on Bury Place and selected one of the images for which I had begrudged the money a few years earlier. I still thought of her vaguely as *the goddess* – not yet assigning to her the dignity of a name. Indeed, it was not I who assigned the name *Hat-hor* to the image I bought. It was the shopkeeper who did so – articulating the name correctly with a hard *T*, followed by a distinct *H* sound. (English people usually pronounce the *ath* as they would in the word *maths* – this is the reason for my hyphenating the two syllables, when writing the goddess' name.)

As soon as he pronounced her name, I recognised that Hat-hor was indeed the goddess to whom my devotions must be addressed. There was an instant sense of rightness – and it seemed strange that I had not already named her for myself.

Names and the process of naming are important. This is emphasised in the myth of Isis and Ra, in which Isis gains power over the sun god by learning his secret name.

It may seem incongruous that a shopkeeper performed the naming. The sage Ptahhotep tells that good speech is as hidden as green stone (perhaps malachite, possibly emeralds) – yet it may be found with the serving women at the grindstones. The shopkeeper may have been passing on an identification made by the maker of the image. In naming her, he might have been acting as an agent of the goddess. (Indeed, whether he viewed his role thus or not, he *was* acting as her agent in distributing her images.) His correct pronunciation of her name marks him as no ignorant man.

I took the image home and set her up on the desk by my bed. But how does one set up an acquaintance with a goddess? Twice a day – morning and evening – I contemplated the image, attempting to clear my mind as I did so (not always successfully).

In my first prayers (when my cat was ill), I had attempted to speak to the goddess. It was some while before I felt able to presume to do this in my twice daily ritual. When I did summon that presumption, it was to praise the goddess, rather than to ask for favours. Nor, at first, did I attempt to address her in English, as I had done before. It seemed more respectful to attempt to articulate phrases from the ancient language of Egypt. A problem with this is that no one knows exactly how the language was pronounced. The Egyptians did not write the vowels. We know that the Egyptian word often translated as *beautiful* or *perfect* was comprised of the three consonants *nfr* in that order. To make this pronounceable, it is conventionally rendered as *nefer* – as in such names as *Nefertiti* and *Nefertari*. Such renditions as *nefer* are essentially unsatisfactory modern artifices, but – for all of that – such forms as *netjeret neferet* (perfect or beautiful goddess) seemed preferable to addressing the goddess in English.

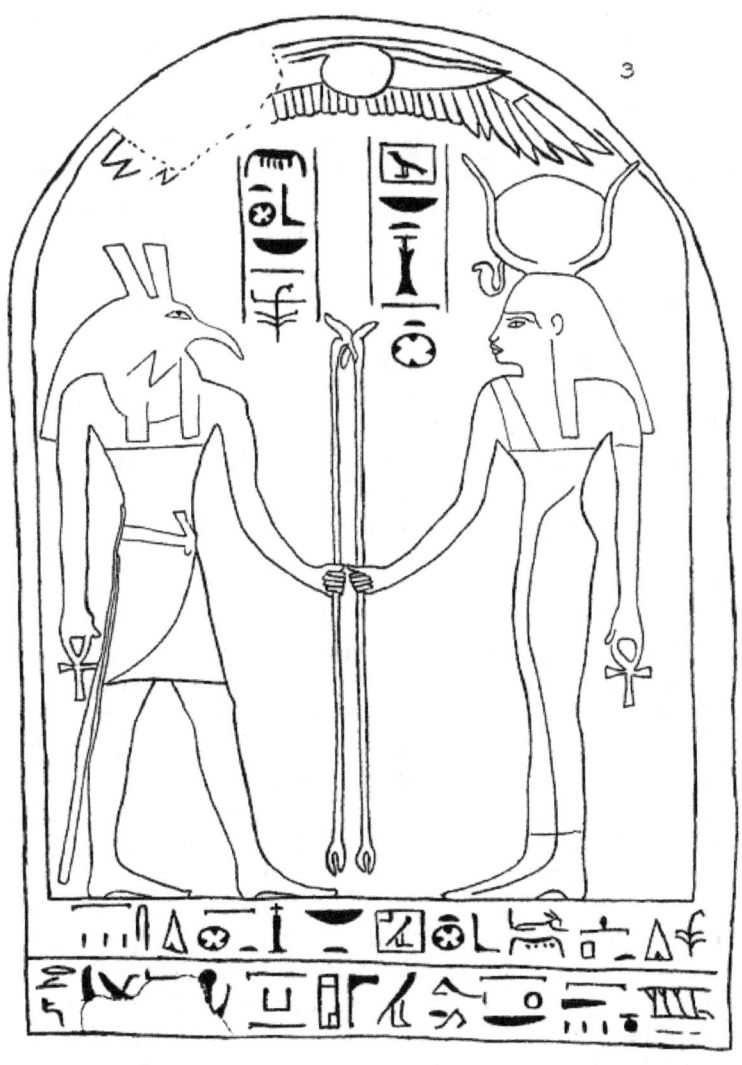

Linguistic philosophy, deconstructive criticism and holy puns

Some have degrees in English, but I wouldn't be in their socks
'Cos I was taught philosophy by Jeremy Roxbee-Cox

It will take me a while to reach linguistic philosophy, deconstructive criticism or holy puns – but the circuitous route I took towards the study of philosophy seems significant.

I did a degree in philosophy at Lancaster University. My journey towards that end started to be set, aged five, on my first day at Infants School. On that day, I was placed in lower stream. The only basis for this – of which I can conceive – is that the more smartly dressed kids were placed in the upper stream, and the scruffier ones in the lower. I remained in the B stream throughout Infants and Junior School. A few children were promoted or demoted between the streams – perhaps one or two of them a year – but I was not one of them. The most extraordinary part of this, it now seems to me, came in my third year at Junior School (aged ten). Without any warning or explanation, I was taken from my class one day and put into a different one. My promotion (if it is to be regarded as such) was not from 3B to 3A – but to 4B. In other words, I was transferred to the year above me, rather than to the upper form of my year. I remained in form 4B for about a year and a half. Perhaps my parents had some kind of explanation for this. If so, they never passed it on to me. (And they are now dead [as – in all probability – are my teachers] so the reason for my transfer from 3B to 4B is unknowable.)

The long-term significance of being placed in the B stream was that it meant failing the eleven-plus exam. We B stream kids were simply not taught everything we needed to know in order to pass the eleven-plus. An example that remains with me is that the exam included sums involving decimal fractions. Those are not difficult – nor did I ever have trouble with decimals – but, in order to do the sums, I would have had to have known the significance of the dots in the figures. No word of this had been passed to the B stream. Essentially – on my first day in Infants School it was decided that I would fail my eleven-plus and go to Secondary Modern, rather than Grammar School.

One of my memories of Junior School days concerns being preoccupied by abstruse questions – and frustration because I didn't have the vocabulary to the express the questions. A specific memory is of being on the cliffs at Leigh-on-Sea with Wendy, my second oldest sister – and trying to express one of these questions to her. It was something to do with *how do I know that I am me* – but that wasn't quite it. My vexation at not being able to express exactly what I meant remains as a vivid recollection. I now think that these questions were philosophical – questions to do with personal identity and the theory of knowledge.

My Secondary Modern School, like the Infants and the Juniors, streamed the pupils – and I was again placed in the lower stream. I suppose that the decision was again made on scruffiness, which I will not deny. The only position of responsibility I achieved at Secondary Modern was ink monitor. This involved going round the class rooms with a huge bottle of ink – at least a gallon of the stuff. The position required a staid but scruffy child. Staid because of the potential mayhem inherent in a gallon school ink. Scruffy because the ink monitor was inevitably inky.

Scruffy but staid, I was now doing well in the half yearly school exams. The headmaster – at some point – asked whether I'd like to go up to the A stream. I said that I'd rather not (because I disliked the A form children, who seemed snobby to me) – so I remained in the B form. That decision affected my future options in that the A steam did French, but the B stream didn't. Possibly, had I entered the A stream, I would not have read philosophy at university – but I anticipate.

I did very well in the Southend-on-Sea Secondary Schools Leaving Certificate exams. That fact, and my parents' willingness to support me for a few more years, enabled me to attend Southend-on-Sea Municipal College where I studied for 'O' and then 'A' level exams. The college offered a choice between what it termed the Science and Commerce Departments. The 'arts' subjects offered by the Commerce Department appealed to me more than the science package – so I took that option. The fact that subjects labeled as *arts* by universities were regarded as *commerce* by the college may say something about the ethos of the institution. On the other hand, it may merely have been to avoid confusion – the college also had an Art Department concerned with the likes of drawing and painting.

I would have loved to have been an art student, but didn't feel that I had the talent – probably not realising the extent to which techniques can be taught.

The Commerce Department 'O' Level courses included French, but everyone else (from A forms of Secondary Modern schools) had been studying French for the last four years – I had not. After a short struggle, I dropped the subject. In some ways, that was a good thing. It gave me some free time in the middle of Southend-on-Sea. I took to sitting in the reference library where, amongst other things, I widened my acquaintance with the culture of ancient Egypt. In other ways, dropping French was not a good thing – it would subsequently reduce my options.

Another subject with which I struggled was maths. The rest of the class had already made the acquaintance of algebra and trigonometry – more A form material – I had not. These branches of mathematics were never properly explained to me. When my work in arithmetic proved to be much better than in algebra and trigonometry, the lecturer seemed to assume that I had cheated. At the end of the first term, the lecturer suggested that I should drop maths, and I readily agreed. More free time, further reduced options.

I never took O Level exams in maths, a language or a science. When I came to apply for a place at university, I discovered that these lacks meant that I had the basic entry qualifications for only five universities in the whole of England. But for these reduced options, I don't suppose that I would have applied to Lancaster University, and very likely would never have encountered linguistic philosophy. One could say that my childhood scruffiness was instrumental in this academic development.

My application was not to the philosophy department, but to read politics with a history minor. In fact, when I applied to university, I had not the least idea as to what philosophy was. But the word *philosophy* struck me as a grand one – and I put myself down to study it as a throw-away first year only subject.

In the event, I found philosophy a lot easier than the two other disciplines for which I had enrolled – and I wasn't keen on working any harder than necessary. Also, I liked the philosophy department staff better than the staff of either of the other departments. Although the philosophy professor (who reminded me of an Indian army colonel) could be intimidating, the lecturers at his disposal often seemed engagingly of another world. They included the kind of men who step backwards into waste paper baskets, or attempt to remove projected images by rubbing the screen with an eraser. The ethics lecturer thought it outrageous that his union was demanding pay rises as, he felt, university lecturers were already over-paid. For such reasons as this, I transferred to the philosophy department – and gained a degree in that discipline.

It happens less now, but people often used to ask me what philosophy is. One way I attempted to explain it is to say that – if one takes the whole of human knowledge, then removes all of the other subjects in the curriculum – then what is left is philosophy. It seeks to ask the fundamental underlying questions – the questions to which we usually assume that we know the answers. For example, the discipline of history seeks to answer the question *what happened in the past?* The question *Is it possible to know what happened in the past?* belongs to philosophy. There is also an intermediate question *What kind of evidence is acceptable for us to assert that something happened in the past?* that spans the grey area between history and philosophy.

Traditionally, philosophical questions have been assumed to be questions about the world – albeit often an abstract version of the world (concerned with concepts, rather than with physical things). Linguistic philosophy, which is central to philosophy as I was taught it, regards philosophical questions as being about language, rather than about the world. The question *Is it possible to know what happened in the past?* could be re-phrased by a linguistic philosopher as *What do we mean by the phrase 'knowing what happened in the past'?*

It has been said (although I'm not sure who said it) that there are two kinds of philosophy. One of them says nothing about everything and the other says everything about nothing. Linguistic philosophy seems to be firmly in the camp of saying everything about nothing. I am reminded of the deconstructive school of literary criticism. Rather than focus on the broad sweep of the texts it considers, it examines and deconstructs key words and phrases. The objective is:

...to refuse the fixity of connotation and to refuse textual closure, to prize open the text to reveal what it won't say, what it cannot say, to make it mean differently.

Berkeley Kaite: *Pornography and Difference.* Indiana University Press, 1995 pp x-xi.

It is tempting to dismiss these approaches in a couple of sentences. They don't seem to take us very far in furthering our understanding of anything. Or, if we do learn anything, it will probably have to do with not wasting our time on academic writings that embrace these concepts.

Yet words are important. Without them, I could not have framed the thoughts I have been trying to express – much less written them down for you to read. The importance of words is, in a Christian context, emphasised by the beginning of St John's gospel: *In the beginning was the word...*

Names are words. In Kemetic myth, the importance of names is emphasised when Isis gains power over Ra by tricking him into revealing his secret name.

Words are, in origin, breath. When we speak, we modify our breathing to make deliberate meaningful sounds. Breath is the stuff of life. We can differentiate between the living and the dead by holding a mirror close to the mouth to see whether it becomes clouded with breath. Breath is fluid – it is here and it is gone. It is the magic of writing that it makes breath solid, it allows us to freeze and preserve that which separates the living from the dead. The life force of those whose bodies have crumbled to dust thousands of years ago can be seen carved in stone or inked on papyrus. My position of responsibility, at school, turns out to be powerful of magics. As ink monitor, I carried the fluid that gives flesh to our breath. It placed me in the following of Thoth, the god associated with (amongst other things) writing and magic.

When I started to read ancient Egyptian religious texts in reliable (and annotated) modern translation, the thing to surprise me most was their containing so many puns and plays on words. I was aged in my 50s when I made this discovery, although I had been looking at Kemetic texts in translation since my late teens. Indeed, in my late 20s, I had taught myself to read Middle Egyptian from Gardiner's *Grammar*. My grasp of the language, alas, was never sufficiently good to follow puns.

Some of the translations at which I looked, if it comes to that, were the work of men whose knowledge of the language was never sufficiently good to follow puns. I use the word *men* advisedly because the older translators were predominantly male. That has now changed – these days, probably the best general anthology of ancient Egyptian writings in translation is Miriam Lichtheim's three volume *Ancient Egyptian Literature* published between 1973 and 1980 (see the bibliography).

If one looks at an old and unannotated translation such as Budge's version of *The Book of the Dead* (strangely still in print long after the appearance of Faulkner's translations of these texts) the puns form incomprehensible passages. Probably there are those who prefer the texts to remain incomprehensible, even when translated into English. After all, strange non sequiturs seem to have a gravitas that puns lack. That said, if we recall that words are important – and that words are breath – it may be that puns take on some importance. A word is a meaningful breath and, if that breath holds more than one meaning, it may be doubly or triply important. Double meanings, and ambiguity in general, are an important element in poetry. Indeed, the word *ambiguity* seems to hold a lot more importance – and significance – than the word *pun*. Multiple meanings, which are what puns are, may be regarded as a reflection of the ambiguity of the observable world – and observable universe. The use of holy puns can, then, be regarded as a sign of the ambiguity of all that we behold, of the doubt we must feel in beholding it, and of the fluidity of our interpretations of the objects (and seeming-objects) we behold. (Or, at least, our interpretations will remain fluid if we are wise – but that is the subject of the next section.)

Phenomenology, the Harper's Song and Akh

Whilst linguistic philosophy ruled the roost (and perhaps still rules it – I neither know nor care) with British academics, a quite different approach was popular on the continent. That approach is phenomenology, a set of ideas that were never mentioned in my philosophy courses. In fact, I didn't encounter phenomenology until more than twenty-five years after graduation. In view of the importance placed on sex in Kemetic belief, it may be significant that it was sex that led me to phenomenology (however improbable that sounds).

Having written that, I find myself imagining – amid a series of orgasmic cries – someone yelling *Philosophise me baby!* I am tempted to pretend that was the way of it, but no...

I was involved in a sexual relationship that ended badly, at least as far as I was concerned. It would almost certainly have been better (for me) had my former partner not taken up with my flat mate. As it was, I was left feeling that I needed some help in sorting my head. With that in mind, I managed to secure low cost limited session counselling.

At the end of my six allocated counselling sessions, I felt that I had started a process of self reconstruction – but by no means completed it. My preference would have been to take up further counselling, but I was unemployed and could not afford to do so. I now view that as fortunate. Experience suggests to me that counselling is often abusive – and that extended counselling is probably always so.

Reviewing my options, it seemed to me that training to become a counsellor would suit both my objectives and my pocket. Being unemployed, I was entitled to a concessionary rate on the course fees. In the event, I didn't need to pay for even that – my father was eager to pay – seeing it as a route back into employment for me.

In the event, my father's expectations were justified. I never secured paid work as a counsellor, but being on a counselling course proved instrumental in finding employment in care work. The skills I learnt on the course weren't very useful in my job – rather, my being offered the work followed from everyone concerned having unrealistic estimations of counselling and counselling courses. (The unrealistic estimations included me, my father and my employers.) For all of that, I shouldn't complain. It did the trick. I had a job and, even if it wasn't a good job, already having a job is the best qualification in a quest for employment.

It's a bit like seeking a large loan – the best qualification is to have lots of money already.

Another benefit of the counselling course is that it brought phenomenology to my attention. Phenomenology is a set of philosophical ideas. It may be interesting that I did a degree in philosophy without once encountering so much as the word *phenomenology*, but discovered it on a course with a non-philosophical remit. I was going to write that it was *strange* that I encountered phenomenology in a non-philosophical context, but on reflection it seems typical of the way things are, and thus not strange at all.

The first year course work on counselling was divided into two discrete units – skills and theory. The skills unit was concerned with the practicalities of counselling – distinguishing, for example, between appropriate and inappropriate, useful and less useful responses to a client. The theory unit dealt with ideas about what makes people tick (and, on that basis, what interventions are likely to be useful and/or appropriate). We started by looking at Freud, then Jung, Klein, Rogers and Adler in that order. After that, we moved on to theories that do not carry an individual's name – starting with Systems Theory. At the very end came Existentialism – something on which I had started to read about six months before. I had been converted by a single sentence which sparked a moment approaching enlightenment. (A bit like a Zen utterance, perhaps.) It was this:

The person is a constant state of becoming.
(Emmy Van Deurzen-Smith in *Individual Therapy: a handbook.*)

It is possible that this was a misprint because the next edition of the book changed it to:

The person is in a constant state of becoming.

It seems to me that Emmy Van Deurzen-Smith was right the first time. We are not *in* the process – we *are* the process. When I first read these words, they sparked what felt (as I have said) almost like Zen instant enlightenment. A great *Yes!* arose instantly within me. It was only years later – reading Erik Hornung's *Conceptions of God in Ancient Egypt* – that I realised how well the process of becoming fitted with a Kemetic worldview. (The section in question is *The challenge of the nonexistent* – pages 172-185.) Herr Hornung draws out a number of interesting and important points – one of them being the Kemetic equation of the unchanging with the nonexistent. Everything is either a process of change – or it does not exist. To change is to be, to be is to change. Change is being, being is change.

I am put in mind, here, of a Christian poster I saw a little while before I read Herr Hornung's remarks on the nonexistent. If my memory serves, it read *Jesus Christ is the same yesterday, today and forever*. I found the poster troubling at the time – a wrongness about the concept of the unchanging that I could not quite pin down. Reading *Conceptions of God in Ancient Egypt*, I encountered another moment of enlightenment. The poster had been proclaiming the nonexistence of Jesus Christ. Well – as such, that doesn't bother me a great deal. To rephrase slightly the words of Jesus, *forgive them, Lord, they know not what they say* – although, as a devotee of Hat-hor, I prefer *forgive them, Lady, they know not what they say*. There is something frightful in asserting that the being who lies at the core of one's belief system is nonexistent.

After the first year of my counselling course, attempting to explore existentialism in more depth, I found a book called *The Interpreted World* by Ernesto Spinelli. This amplifies the idea of *the person is a constant state of becoming* as:

...the 'self' that we interpret and believe in at any given moment... is both temporary and, at best, a partial expression of an infinity of potential interpreted selves.

The word *interpreted* in both the title of Mr Spinelli's book, and in this quotation, lies at the heart of phenomenology – the approach to belief underlying existentialism. Phenomenology is based upon the idea that, although there is such a thing as objective reality, it is essentially unknowable. We filter – and interpret – the world through our assumptions, preconceptions and prejudices.

Although we cannot truly know objective reality, we can approach doing so in employing the phenomenological method. The method has three rules:

The first is to attempt, as far as possible, to be aware of our assumptions, preconceptions and prejudices – and to seek to put them to one side (or to 'bracket' them).

The second is to describe rather than to explain. To attempt to explain is to interpret.

The third is – at least initially – to treat everything (no matter how trivial-seeming) as of equal importance. Discounting something (as unimportant or irrelevant) is part of the process of applying our filters to the world.

Applying the phenomenological method, of course, does not – and cannot – give us certainty. Phenomenology is, then, a philosophy of doubt and uncertainty. It may seem at odds with religions of any kind. It seems characteristic of religions (in general) to treat of certainties in areas in which it is hard to see how anyone could be certain. The Church of England funeral service, for example, mentions *the sure and certain hope* of something or other. Is it the resurrection of the body, or some other piece of afterlife business? I forget – but I have been struck by the phrase and have marveled that anyone could even pretend to be either sure or certain of such a thing. I also note the redundancy of *sure and certain* – surely either word would do on its own. Perhaps the redundancy betrays an unacknowledged doubt.

The Kemetic view, by contrast, is capable of admitting doubt. There is a class of ancient Egyptian poems known as *Harpers' songs* (evidently to be sung whilst playing the harp). The best known of them survives in two New Kingdom copies, but – in view of its language – is clearly older. The preamble to the song states that it was inscribed in the tomb of King Intef – a name held by several kings of the Eleventh and Seventeenth Dynasties. Although this original has not survived (or is not known to have done so) there is no reason to doubt (beyond reasons to doubt almost *everything*) that it came from a Middle Kingdom royal tomb.

Here is the central portion of the song – in both the 1920s translation I first read aged (I think) 19, and in Miriam Lichtheim's excellent modern translation. I include the Erman/Blackman version because it is the text that influenced me in my late teens and early twenties. Miriam Lichtheim's translation is not only informed by modern scholarship, but is better English. I must have been aware of some shortcomings in Blackman's English version – not long after encountering it for the first time – I went to the trouble of producing my own English rendition at the age of 20 (rewriting the translation, long before I learnt Egyptian).

Aylward M. Blackman's 1927 rendition into English of Adolf Erman's 1923 translation: *The Literature of the Ancient Egyptians* **(1927).**

They that build houses, their habitations are no more. What hath been done with them?
I have heard the discourses of Imhotep and Hardedef, with whose words men speak everywhere – what are their habitations (now)? Their walls are destroyed, their habitations are no more, as if they had never been.
None cometh from thence that he may tell us how they fare, that he may tell us what they need, that he may set our heart at rest (?), until we also go to the place whither they are gone.
Be glad, that thou mayest cause thine heart to forget that men will (one day) beatify thee. Follow thy desire, so long as thou livest. Put myrrh on thine head, clothe thee in fine linen, and anoint thee with the genuine marvels of the things of the god.

Miriam Lichtheim's 1973 translation: *Ancient Egyptian Literature Vol. I: The Old and Middle Kingdoms* **(1973).**

(Yet) those who build tombs,
Their places are gone,
What has become of them?
I have heard the words of Imhotep and Hardedef,
Whose sayings are recited whole.
What of their places?
Their walls are crumbled,
Their places are gone,
As though they had never been!
None comes from there,
To tell us of their state,
To tell us of their needs,
To calm our hearts
Until we go where they have gone!
Hence rejoice your heart!
Forgetfulness profits you,
Follow your heart as long as you live!
Put myrrh on your head,
Dress in fine linen,
Anoint yourself with oils fit for a god.

In other words, as we don't know what will happen to us after death, we should enjoy our lives while we can. I am unaware of anything more sensible said on the matter in the thousands of years since the harpers' songs were written.

Not only does this express doubt concerning the afterlife, but it was evidently inscribed in a royal tomb. If this was an individual view – let alone considered an heretical one – finding it in a king's tomb would be very surprising. The fate of a private individual might hinge upon the decoration and inscriptions of her or his tomb – but the fate of the entire nation might hinge upon those in the king's tomb. This distinction is clearly evident in the eighteenth dynasty tombs at Thebes. The paintings in the kings' tombs are stiff and formal, religious scenes as far as I can see unrelieved by humour or observations of life. They are – essentially – only of interest to scholars. By contrast, those in private tombs are full of life and detail. Repeatedly, we see the household cat under the tomb owner's chair. We see girls fighting in the fields at harvest time. An especial favourite of mine is found the tomb of Intef (Theban tomb 155). A party of men are delivering wine to a storehouse. The store keeper is evidently slow to answer the knock. The man knocking says that the store keeper is asleep; the man immediately behind says that he's drunk from the wine. The store keeper, not yet having arisen, and holding his head with one hand, protests that he hasn't been asleep. Most likely, I suppose, he has been overcome by wine fumes. Such individuality would not have been acceptable in the tomb of the king.

The doubt about the afterlife raised by the harpers' songs seems to me to have parallels with phenomenology which is, essentially, a philosophy of doubt. The Egyptian concept of *akh* – while not directly concerned with doubt – may also have implications relevant to phenomenology.

The Egyptian word *akh* is difficult to translate into English. In *A Concise Dictionary of Middle Egyptian*, Raymond Faulkner defines it as a verb *to be or become a spirit* – or, as an adjective, either as *glorious, splendid* or as *beneficial, useful, profitable*. As an adjective, it combines the practical (*useful*) with the spiritual (*glorious*). That may seem surprising. Two variants spelt differently (but still *akh*, and most certainly the same word) are defined respectively as *spirit* and *the spirit state* – which variants shift the balance of senses in favour of the spiritual.

The related word *akhet* shifts the balance back towards the practical – meaning *what is good, profitable, useful*. *Akhu*, by contrast, combines both *–power* of a god or *mastery* over work.

It seems to me that there is something here that comes close to prefiguring phenomenology. Perceiving reality is to discover truth. Our profitable or useful assumptions bring us towards the truth – which is splendid or glorious. What is neither profitable nor useful will lead us from the splendour of the truth. In this regard, Henri Frankfort wrote of *akh*:

...it may mean "to be agreeable," "to be advantageous," but also "to be effective, splendid, sacred, transfigured" – meanings which find their common root in the concept of harmony with the divine order of the universe.

Henri Frankfort *Ancient Egyptian Religion an interpretation*. Dover Books edition pp 63-64.

Looking forward, the divine order of the universe must bring us, next, to *ma'at...* Looking back to an earlier part of this essay, effective spirits, *akhu*, are surely the personalities we have already encountered in images, books and a rose bush embodying the *akh* of a lady's late husband.

Ma'at

*But, as both are daughters of Re, Maat cannot be separated from Hathor.
The guiding influence of Maat needs the energising vitality and life-blood
of Hathor to maintain her way of the world.*

Alison Roberts: *My Heart My Mother. Death and Rebirth in Ancient
Egypt.* Northgate Publishers, 2000. p 123.

Ma'at is, like *akh*, an Egyptian word that is difficult to translate into
English. I place the apostrophe in the middle, not because there is an
elision, but to make it clear that ma'at is a two syllable word. It is quite
often written *maat*, which I used to pronounce as *mart*. It was not until I
read Gardiner's *Egyptian Grammar* that I realised the word should have
two syllables. Since then, I have pronounced it as though it were spelled
may-at, with the first *a* long and the second *a* short. No doubt this
pronunciation doesn't correspond with the way it was voiced in ancient
times – but it is certainly better than *mart*.

I try to take care with the pronunciation of *ma'at* because it is, perhaps,
the most important of all concepts for Kemetic religion. This conception
is sufficiently important to regard Ma'at as a goddess in her own right. In
the most usual iconography, Ma'at is represented as a woman with a
feather on her head.

In the religion of ancient Hellas, there would be nothing remarkable in
regarding Ma'at as a goddess. The Hellenes regularly regarded important
bodies or concepts as deities. Thus we have (for example) Helios as a
sun god; Selene as a moon goddess and Hypnos as the god of sleep while
helios, *selene* and *hypnos* are the ordinary Hellenic words for *sun*, *moon*
and *sleep*. This was not the way of the Egyptians. The most important
solar deity is Ra – but *ra* is not an ordinary word for *sun*. As I have
already observed:

People sometimes ask me what is Hat-hor the goddess of? *If she were a
Hellenic goddess, for example, I would probably be able to give a short
meaningful answer.* **Question:** What is Aphrodite the goddess of?
Answer: Love. *By and large with the Egyptian deities, and certainly in
the case of Hat-hor, such an answer is more misleading than helpful.*

A good reason that the Egyptian word for *sleep* is not a divine name is
that there is no god (or goddess) of sleep in Kemetic religion. Indeed, in
the paragraph before last, I was careful to write *the most important solar*

deity is Ra, rather than the simpler (but misleading) statement that *the sun god is Ra*. Hat-hor is, amongst other things, a solar deity hence the frequently seen iconography in which she is crowned with the sun disk. The relationship between deity and the sun is complex.

All of this being so, when the concept of *ma'at* is also the goddess Ma'at, something special is at work. What, then, is *ma'at*?

Like most untranslatable words, it does get translated – usually as *truth* or *justice*. For example, in the texts generally known as *The Book of the Dead* (the Egyptian title is very different – *Peret em Heru* – which translates as *Coming Forth by Day*) the heart of the deceased is weighed against the feather of ma'at. In this context, the translation is likely to be *the feather of truth*. This rendition is at best inexact, and may be misleading.

A closer approximation to the sense of *ma'at* is *divine order*. I am not sure whether referring to *the feather of divine order* is likely to convey much to most people. *The feather of truth* does seem to read better in English.

One great advantage in the translation as *divine order* is that this makes it clear that *ma'at* is, fundamentally, a religious concept. Another advantage is that order and balance are essential to the concept of *ma'at*. *Ma'at* concerns order, balance and harmony between the stars, and between people. It is, simultaneously a religious, cosmic and moral concept.

Ma'at, indeed, extends beyond the religious, cosmic and moral to questions of etiquette. Some commentators on Egyptian wisdom literature have expressed puzzlement at the way in which these texts mix rules of etiquette with moral guidelines. The matter becomes comprehensible when one realises that both have their basis in *ma'at*. Polite behaviour facilitates order, balance and harmony between people.

The concept of *ma'at* also translates readily into the field of ecology. Ecological balance is a matter of balance between species, and between those species and the environments in which they live. This clearly has a kinship with the balance between the stars, which is most certainly a matter of *ma'at*. Ecology is not, in itself, an ancient Egyptian concept, but the way in which it slots so readily into Kemetic ideas demonstrates how adaptable those conceptions are. It may also form another example of the ease with which Kemetic religion fits with rationalism.

Indeed, ideas about ecology may prove helpful in illuminating the concept of *ma'at*. In hunter-gather societies, humans (still in their natural ecological niche) must have automatically been in a state of *ma'at* – just as other animals are. No doubt this is not only true historically, but true of the few hunter-gatherers who remain. It is our removal from our ecological niche, via agriculture, into civilisation that removes us from *ma'at* – and means that we (alone of all creatures on earth) need to take action to approach a state of *ma'at*.

This is not to say that there is anything wrong, as such, in agriculture and civilisation. These things emerge from instincts – to do with survival of the individual and of the species – common to every creature on earth. Our removal from the life of the hunter gatherer enables us to breed in greater numbers and to survive (individually) for much longer. It is, therefore, in accordance with the basic aims of life. It is, in a sense, natural – but that is not to say that it is without problems. It places us out of balance with the divine and natural order – but, in a Kemetic Rationalist view, it is possible for us to regain that balance.

In framing this view of *ma'at*, ecology and the place of people in the world, I have created an example of Kemetic rationalism. It combines ancient Kemetic concepts with modern rational ones in what I trust to be a harmonious way, doing little violence to either. More – ancient and modern elements illuminate and clarify one another.

Some might, contrariwise, see my ecological view of *ma'at* as contradicting ancient concepts, because the Egyptians tended to view wild nature as an aspect of chaos. Clearly, chaos – *isfet* in Egyptian – is the opposite of order, but *isfet* and *ma'at* are not necessarily or ultimately separable. Not only is *ma'at* order, but there is an order in the balance between *ma'at* and *isfet*:

The crux of the ancient Egyptian system of beliefs was the relationship between order (maat) and chaos (isfet). Although a state of order was considered to be the ideal, it was acknowledged that an opposing yet interdependent state of chaos must exist in order for equilibrium to be achieved.

Lucia Gahlin: *Egypt Gods, Myths and Religion.* Hermes House, 2004. p86.

There are balances between balances, and within balances – and the power Hat-hor moves within them as an essential force. The drunkenness (*tekhi*, in Egyptian) associated with Hat-hor is not at all the same thing as chaos (*isfet*) but there are also balances to be struck between *tekhi* and *ma'at*:

...Maat can only truly guide if united with the volatile Hathor. Both goddesses are 'daughters of Re'; and both are shown standing erect at the prow of the sun-boat during the solar journey – one goddess crowned with her characteristic feather, the other with her horned headdress. The son of a wise old priest of Amun at Karnak succinctly sums up this paradox of 'sober drunkenness' as he prays to the retinue of Re, asking for their blessings on his father:

Let his hands receive your offerings,
For see he has pure hands.
Let his mouth be filled with provisions,
For see he spoke the truth (Maat) in his sobriety.
Let him drink from your libations,
For see he loves drunkenness.

His prayer displays a profound awareness that Maat and Hathor, order and drunkenness, are both needed in the solar circuit.

Alison Roberts: *Hathor Rising. The Serpent Power of Ancient Egypt.* Northgate Publishers, 1995. pp 34-36.

Golden Goddess

Starting

For such a slender book, this has taken a long while to complete – at least five years, and I think longer. The slow process reminds me of the even slower development I described, of my stepping to meet Hat-hor.

The earliest version of the essay runs to only four pages. Looking at this text today, for the first time in years, I'm surprised to discover that more than half of it is material that doesn't appear in this much longer version. The excised pages centre upon a precise description of my twice daily (morning and evening) ritual in which I devote myself Hat-hor. Over the ensuing years, the rituals have changed somewhat, evolved. It would be possible for me to set down an account of the rituals in their present form. I could even, using the early text, provide some history of their evolution. On reflection, doing anything of the sort seems neither useful nor interesting. My twice daily encounters with the goddess are personal. It would be wrong to claim for them any measure of authority. A person wishing to follow in my path should make her or his own approaches to divinity, and certainly not copy me.

Indeed, my approach is based upon an explicit rejection of organised religion. Not only are organised religions, in my experience, corrupt – but they inevitably assume a rigidity, a fixity that is a denial of the goddess' fluidity.

What I can do is to suggest how the reader might start to approach the goddess. My abandoned account of the rituals began with this:

My twice daily (morning and evening) prayers are directed to Hat-hor. I purchased a small statuette of the goddess from a shop near the British Museum. This image forms the focus of my prayers – a representation (image) of the goddess to whom the prayers are directed.

The shop near the British Museum was called, if I remember correctly, *The Egyptian Bazaar*. Subsequently, the premises changed hands, and sold Hellenic items. The last time I walked along that street, it had become a small beauty parlour. My sense was that it had sold what I needed to buy, at the right time, and – having done so – the building had moved on. Similarly, it seems to me, if the reader needs an image of the goddess, she will be available.

Having secured my image, the earliest forms of my rituals require little explanation. Twice a day, I stared at the goddess' image, attempting – as

I did so – to empty my mind of its usual clutter. Having done this for several months, additional business occurred to me – raising my hands in adoration, speaking to the goddess. Some such business soon felt wrong, and I abandoned it. Other words and gestures felt right – I continued and developed them. Slowly, my rituals emerged, changing and continuing to change. Meeting the goddess is a process.

For me, as writer, this essay has been a long process, which now appears to approach its ending. Once the text turns into ink on paper, it will have reached fixity. Yet for you, the reader, perhaps it may continue to be fluid. A starting, or at least a continuing, rather than an ending. The following words now strike me as more significant than they seemed when I first quoted them:

...to refuse the fixity of connotation and to refuse textual closure, to prize open the text to reveal what it won't say, what it cannot say, to make it mean differently.

Berkeley Kaite: *Pornography and Difference.* Indiana University Press, 1995 pp x-xi.

We will do well to bear in mind the importance of change. To be fixed is not to be at all. As I observed on page 16 of this essay:

Deities – and the world in general – are not constant or unchanging. They are renewed, and the process of renewal is essentially sexual – and requires both sexes. Not to change is not to exist. Not to have sexual processes is not to exist.

By way of conclusion, I will quote again page 162 of *Sacred Sexuality in Ancient Egypt* by Ruth Schumann Antelme and Stephane Rossini (Inner Traditions, 2001):

Hathor's secrets are numerous, varied, and often strange, but all derive from the first becoming, the divine creation of the universe, and commingle, on the terrestrial level, with humanity's history since its inception. Hathor the Golden One, the Sovereign of Love, and Lady of Death, Mistress of Drunkenness, the ravaging Distant One and the tender Bastet, joyous Mistress of music and dance, the generous Celestial Cow, lady of the Vulva and womb of the world, Ra's burning eye, his untameable daughter, Uraeus who defends her father and protects the king, the Unique One who is always everywhere and nowhere, as ungraspable as love.

Further Reading.

I've changed my mind about this bibliography several times – in regard to its aims, format and size. Taking only the first of these, I considered making it a list of the books that had shaped this essay. Another, more modest, idea was to set out the books I'd actively consulted in the process of writing this. Finally, I've decided on a third, more useful (*akh*), list – the books which, I think, will be of most use in further exploring the themes I've taken up.

A word of caution. In consulting books of the subject of ancient Egypt, it is generally better to avoid the works of E. A. Wallis Budge. In spite of still being easily available, Mr Budge's books are not only out of date, but were (at best) carelessly written. They contain a great number of errors.

By contrast, I especially recommend the following titles:

Jan Assman. *The Mind of Egypt. History and Meaning in the Time of the Pharaohs*. Harvard University Press, 1996. An essential commentary on Egyptian ideals, values and thought.

Adolf Erman. *The Ancient Egyptians. A Sourcebook of Their Writings*. Translated into English by Aylward M. Blackman. Methuen, 1927 (as *The Literature of the Ancient Egyptians*). Harper Torchbooks, 1966. Some of these aging translations still have a lot of power, but consult Miriam Lichtheim first.

Henri Frankfort. *Ancient Egyptian Religion. An Interpretation. Columbia University Press, 1948*. Later editions include Harper Torchbook and Dover Books paperbacks. Contains some fascinating insights, particularly those focused upon the concept of *akh*.

Lucia Gahlin. *Egypt Gods, Myths and Religion*. Hermes House, updated edition, 2004. A good place to start. Many illustrations, a pleasure to peruse – and also contains useful insights.

Erik Hornung. *Conceptions of God in Ancient Egypt. The One and the Many*. Translated from the German by John Baines. Cornell University Press, 1982. In my opinion, the best general book on Egyptian (Kemetic) Religion.

Patrick F. Houlihan. *Wit & Humour in Ancient Egypt*. The Rubicon Press, 2001. Entertaining examination of a sometimes overlooked, but important, aspect of Egyptian thought.

Barbara S. Lesko. *The Great Goddesses of Egypt*. University of Oklahoma Press, 1999. Devotes almost 50 pages to Hat-hor. A fine book that delivers what is implied in the title.

Miriam Lichtheim. *Ancient Egyptian Literature*. Three Volumes. University of California Press, 1973, 1976 & 1980. An indispensable collection – a large sampling of ancient Egyptian writings, presented in excellent translations.

Lise Manniche. *Sexual Life in Ancient Egypt*. Kegan Paul, 1987. A highly readable treatment of an important subject, not to be missed.

Geraldine Pinch. *Votive Offerings to Hathor*. Griffith Institute, 1993. A fine scholarly work, not the place to start reading, but of enormous value.

Stephen Quirke. *Egyptian Literature 1800 BC questions and readings*. Golden House Publications, 2004. Parallel no nonsense translations and transliterated Egyptian texts give an unbeatable glimpse of Egyptian literature.

Alison Roberts. *Hathor Rising. The Serpent Power of Ancient Egypt*. Northgate Publishers, 1995.
Alison Roberts. *My Heart My Mother. Death and Rebirth in Ancient Egypt*. Northgate Publishers, 2000. These two books form an excellent account of Hat-hor religion. Indispensable reading.

Ruth Schumann Antelme & Stephane Rossini. *Sacred Sexuality in Ancient Egypt. The Erotic Secrets of the Forbidden Papyrus*. Translated by Jon Graham. Inner Traditions, 2001. An exploration of the Turin erotic papyrus. A work of fundamental importance.

William Kelly Simpson (ed.). *The Literature of Ancient Egypt*. Second Edition. Yale University Press, 1973.
William Kelly Simpson (ed.). *The Literature of Ancient Egypt*. Third Edition. Yale University Press, 2003. In spite of looking to be different editions of the same book, these are really entirely separate. The translations are different, and – in some cases – the works translated are different. The second edition is notable for Raymond Faulker's fine translations. The third edition is much longer, and one of the few places in which one will find *The Book of the Heavenly Cow* translated in its entirety.

Ernesto Spinelli. *The Interpreted World. An Introduction to Phenomenological Psychology*. Sage Publications,1989. A book that had a profound effect on my thinking.

Barbara Watterson. *Gods of Ancient Egypt*. Bramley Books, 1999. A good general introduction to Egyptian goddesses and gods.

Richard H. Wilkinson. *The Complete Gods and Goddesses of Ancient Egypt*. Thames & Hudson, 2003. While I feel that the title overdoes things somewhat, this is a thorough (and well illustrated) treatment of the Egyptian pantheon.

www.ingramcontent.com/pod-product-compliance
Lightning Source LLC
Chambersburg PA
CBHW060643290526
45793CB00001B/381